WITH ALL DUE

RESPECT

WITH ALL DUE

RESPECT

*Defending America with
Grit and Grace*

Nikki R. Haley

St. Martin's Press
New York

First published in the United States by St. Martin's Press,
an imprint of St. Martin's Publishing Group

www.stmartins.com

The opinions and characterizations in this piece are those of the author and do not
necessarily represent those of the U.S. government.

The Library of Congress Cataloging-in-Publication Data is available upon request.

ISBN 978-1-250-26655-2 (hardcover)
ISBN 978-1-250-26656-9 (ebook)

Our books may be purchased in bulk for promotional, educational, or business use.
Please contact your local bookseller or the Macmillan Corporate and Premium Sales
Department at 1-800-221-7945, extension 5442, or by email
at MacmillanSpecialMarkets@macmillan.com.

First Edition: November 2019

10 9 8 7 6 5 4 3 2 1

TO THE PEOPLE OF AMERICA:

I HOPE THIS IS A REMINDER THAT ON OUR

WORST DAY, WE ARE BLESSED TO LIVE IN AMERICA.

Contents

WITH ALL DUE

RESPECT

Prologue

On August 22, 2017, I boarded a flight to Vienna, Austria. It was a flight that almost didn't happen.

I was going to visit the United Nations' agency in charge of nuclear-weapons inspections, the International Atomic Energy Agency (IAEA). As America's ambassador to the United Nations, my mission was to explore Iranian compliance with the nuclear deal that the Obama administration and much of the world had agreed to in 2015.

A month before, in the Oval Office, I had discussed this subject with President Trump. He viewed the Iran deal as deeply flawed and dangerous, and he was frustrated that his national security team had persuaded him to stick with the deal twice already that year. He was looking for a way out.

I agreed with the president. The Iran deal was a disaster for American interests. I told him we needed to lay a stronger public foundation for why we should get out of the deal. He eagerly agreed, saying "Rex [Secretary of State Rex Tillerson] hasn't done a f—ing thing on it. And I'm not going to renew this thing again."

I was excited that the president wanted me to pursue this direction. My first move was going to see the nuclear inspectors in Vienna.

Not everyone in our government liked that idea.

ON A WARM AUGUST NIGHT, shortly after our Oval Office discussion, President Trump, Secretary of State Rex Tillerson, and I were gathered poolside at the president's golf club in Bedminster, New Jersey.

Families relaxed amid harried national security aides. Children ran and jumped in the pool as officials moved from meeting to meeting. And in a cottage down the way, the foreign policy of the nation was being decided.

We were there to talk about North Korea and other national security issues. Joining Secretary Tillerson and me were National Security Advisor H. R. McMaster and brand-new White House Chief of Staff John Kelly. It was no secret that Rex and I had had our differences. But that night they reached what one anonymous White House source would call "World War III levels."

Tensions were already high from an earlier meeting that day. Rex had been arrogant and condescending. He gave off the unmistakable impression that he knew more than everyone else in the room—including the president. And I will confess that I have never been good with people who are so convinced of their superiority that they refuse to hear anyone else out. Dealing with Rex could be exhausting.

Tillerson opposed U.S. withdrawal from the Iran deal, and he was not alone in that view within the administration. My perspective was different. I had been heavily engaged at the UN in negotiating sanctions on the North Korean regime for their nuclear-weapons and ballistic-missile programs. I knew how important it was that the United States send a strong signal to the North Korean dictator Kim Jong Un that we weren't going to accept from his country the kind of deal we had accepted from Iran. If we were serious about ending the North Korean nuclear threat—and we were—we had to let North Korea know what our redlines were. Further, I had seen how Iran had used the weak UN resolution that had embraced the nuclear deal to justify every type of its bad behavior, including the development of ballistic missiles capable of carrying nuclear weapons.

My case to the president was straightforward: The Iran deal had been sold dishonestly to the American people, without any significant debate about its merits. Majorities in both houses of Congress had voted against it. The American people needed to hear why this agreement was bad for our national security, I said.

I told the president of my intention to travel to the IAEA to start the process that he and I had discussed.

At that point, Secretary Tillerson inserted himself into our conversation.

"No, we're not going to do this," he said.

I looked at him, stunned. I wasn't asking for his permission. I was asking the president.

"I have staff in Vienna," he said. "They're meeting with the IAEA. Everything is fine. We don't need to do anything."

I strongly suspected that Rex was making things up as he went along. I had heard nothing about his staff consulting with the IAEA about the Iran deal.

I said, "Rex, why can't I go to Vienna? I just want to ask questions."

"You don't need to," he said. "You need to stay out of it."

I regretted that our disagreement had to play out in front of the president, but I wasn't about to back down. I was a member of the president's cabinet and the National Security Council, just as Rex was. We had already extended the Iran deal twice to give our European allies the chance to demand that Iran change its aggressive behavior. They hadn't. And Iran's violent suppression of the Iranian people and its support for terrorism had only increased since the nuclear deal was signed.

The Iranian regime wasn't becoming less dangerous, it was becoming more so. And I knew the only way to focus the international community on the danger posed by Iran was to threaten the nuclear agreement.

Rex and I continued to argue back and forth. I should stay in my lane, he said. I had no business in the matter. I responded that Iran was in violation of multiple UN Security Council resolutions for its support of terrorism, ballistic-missile launches, and weapons exports. This was most definitely my business.

"Rex, what's wrong if she goes to Vienna?" President Trump said. "I don't think it's a bad thing."

Then the president decided he had had enough.

"You all get together and figure this out," he said.

I had said what I needed to say already—to the president. He had okayed my plan. It would have been great to have Rex on board, but I didn't need his approval, and I wasn't going to wait for it.

Rex and I never agreed on the Iran deal. But within the sixty-day timetable I had promised the president, I did go to Vienna. Two weeks later, I made a major speech outlining the serious problems with the agreement and describing why the president would be justified in abandoning it. On October 13, President Trump de-certified the deal, and on May 8, 2018, he announced the United States was withdrawing from it.

The exchange that August night between Rex and myself at Bedminster was unusual. The president would later say, "I have never seen anybody be treated the way Rex treated Nikki." Even in the Trump administration, this wasn't how policy was typically made. But the incident was also a great snapshot of my relationship with the president. When I had an idea about a direction for U.S. foreign policy—with regard to Iran, Venezuela, North Korea, or elsewhere—I could pick up the phone and call the president. Our communication was nearly constant, and it was straightforward. We didn't always see eye-to-eye. Sometimes I called to privately express my disagreement with a policy. But he always took the call and he always listened. Usually, as in the case of the Iran deal, we agreed.

The result was that I had unusual latitude to operate as U.S. am-bassador to the United Nations. I was free to largely chart my own course—and I did. It was not a typical situation for a UN ambas-sador. But President Trump and I understood each other. I knew my responsibility to act in accordance with his objectives. And he trusted me enough to allow me to be flexible with how I executed his wishes. He also knew I would be honest with him when I dis-agreed, and he appreciated that.

Most of what we did at the UN was consistent with the president's campaign promises and positions. We challenged business as usual in New York and demanded more of a return for America's dispropor-tionate investment in the United Nations, the largest by far of any nation. We renewed and reaffirmed our close relationship with our

friend and ally Israel. We asserted our sovereign right to move the
U.S. embassy to Israel's capital, Jerusalem. We passed three separate
and strong packages of sanctions on North Korea for its nuclear program. That meant doing what had never been done before, bringing
China along. By the end of my term as ambassador, we had sanc-
tioned North Korea more harshly than any country in a generation.

There were other areas in which I regarded my role as filling in
important gaps in the administration's rhetoric and policy. From my
very first appearance in the UN Security Council, we went relentlessly against Russia for its aggression in Ukraine, its illegal seizure
of Crimea, its support for the Syrian dictator Bashar al-Assad, and
its role in chemical-weapons attacks on civilians in Great Britain.

It was never easy dealing with the Russians. Early on, I heard
that the Russian ambassador, a gruff and gregarious party-liner
who has since passed away, named Vitaly Churkin, had told a colleague he didn't think I was very smart. I'm used to being underestimated, so I didn't get angry at Vitaly. I didn't stop working with
him. I didn't care whether the Russians thought I was smart or not.
I had a job to do—to represent the country I loved with strength
and facts. And that's what I did. I wasn't going to be distracted by
insults.

By the time I left the UN, the Russians' perception of me had
changed completely. A member of the Russian delegation confessed
to one of my deputy ambassadors that the Russians would miss me.
"We all wish we could talk like her. I mean, she literally called us
losers today," he said after one of our final Security Council sessions. "How does she get away with saying what she says and still
manage to get her way?"

Human rights was another area in which I felt a special responsibility to speak up. At the root of so many of the conflicts that came to us in the UN Security Council were violations of human rights. The refugee crises created by the war in Syria, the ethnic cleansing in Burma, and conflicts across Africa began with the violation of the rights of ethnic groups or government dissidents. This is something that the dictatorial governments at the United Nations don't like to hear, but it's a fact. The protection of human rights is the protection and preservation of peace and security. We were determined to make this connection, and did so often during my tenure.

For me, human rights have a natural, central place in U.S. foreign policy because they reflect our principles as Americans. When I was governor of South Carolina, we were the first state in the nation to pass a law taking on the anti-Semitic Boycott, Divestment and Sanction (BDS) movement. We stopped using taxpayer funds to do business with any company that discriminates on the basis of race, color, religion, gender, or national origin. I was proud of South Carolinians for acting in defense of our values. I felt the same way at the UN. The American principles of freedom and human dignity are the source of our national greatness and our most powerful foreign-policy instruments. We can't and we shouldn't be the world's nanny or policeman. But we should act abroad in ways that honor our values.

One of the great misconceptions of our time is that a strong, confident America is somehow at odds with the protection of human rights abroad. I reject this notion. I didn't believe it before I came to the UN, and after two years battling with some of the world's most evil regimes, I'm more convinced than ever that American leadership is necessary for a more peaceful and just world. They don't like to admit it, but other countries feel the same way. Many countries never miss the opportunity to publicly run down the United States at the UN. But I can't tell you how many times representatives of these same countries used very different words in private. Time and again they told me that they welcomed—even yearned for—U.S. leadership. They envy our ability to live and speak freely. They admire our principles. And they depend on us to lead the world in accordance with our values.

I look back on my time in the Trump administration, and I see that it was a time when America found her voice again in foreign policy. We regained a confidence and an assertiveness that we had lost.

At least part of the reason for America finding its voice again was that the administration was unafraid to challenge the status quo. I was a foreign-policy novice who faced a learning curve when I became ambassador. I studied a lot before coming to New York. But I purposefully didn't study the United Nations itself, and here's why: I wanted to preserve my ability to see the UN through new eyes, with a fresh perspective.

I looked at the United Nations the way many Americans do, if they look at all. And what I saw was a lot of hypocrisy and dysfunction being tolerated as business as usual. The United States is by far the largest contributor to the United Nations. But what have we been getting for our investment? For decades, countries bad-mouthed us at the United Nations and we did nothing. They ran down our allies and we did nothing. Even countries we consider our friends voted against us or failed to support us when we needed them. Then they turned around and stuck their hands out, expecting foreign aid and other favors from the United States.

The UN is a tough place to work. It is not for the soft of heart. You have to believe in what you're fighting for and never let your guard down. It is a place that does much good in housing refugees and feeding the poor. But it is also a place where the U.S. ambassador can find herself on the losing end of a 189-to-2 vote meant to trash the United States or Israel. It's a place that rises to applaud tyrants scoring cheap political points by bad-mouthing these same countries. It's a place where evil regimes can prevent good people from doing good things through the power of their veto.

I looked to my predecessor, Jeane Kirkpatrick, our UN ambassador under President Ronald Reagan, for guidance on how to navigate these treacherous waters. Not just because she was the lone woman on the Security Council, as I was when I began, but because she cared about the United States' role at the United Nations. She wanted her work there to matter. And she understood the power of her voice.

Ambassador Kirkpatrick understood that it mattered less for the United States to be loved at the United Nations than it mattered to be respected. She once said, "We take the UN very seriously. We notice, we care, we *remember*." I put it a little differently, but it was the same idea. I said we would "have the backs" of those who supported us, and "take the names" of those who didn't. My new colleagues didn't know what to make of it when I said these words on my first day at the UN. And I will confess that I was operating mostly on instinct at that point. I would go on to learn a lot about the world and the power to change it. I would lose some fights. But I never lost sight of the fact that I was speaking for the American people. My voice was their voice. I owed it to them to be principled, strong, and bold.

In the end, the greatest lesson I learned from my time at the United Nations was not about the world, but about America. My travel as ambassador took me to places most Americans will never see. I went to countries where life is cheap, liberty is nonexistent, and happiness is a distant dream. I met with refugees from the conflict in South Sudan, where rape is routinely used as a weapon of war. I visited camps filled with families that fled the conflict in Syria, where the monster President Assad uses chemical weapons to murder innocent children. I've sat in the same hall as North Korean officials who starve their own people to feed their nuclear and missile programs.

There is a growing tendency in American politics to regard other Americans who don't think like we do as not just wrong, but evil. But I have seen true evil. And it has given me a new perspective on America. I wish everyone squabbling on Twitter could see what I have seen. I wish all the students on college campuses who won't tolerate other viewpoints, and members of the media who ostracize public figures for political incorrectness—I wish they could see what I've seen. Because when you've met Chinese ethnic minorities whose relatives are in "re-education" camps because they are not allowed to give their children traditional names or speak their language or practice their religion, it's hard to get emotional about politically incorrect speech. And when you've had a refugee woman tell you about watching soldiers throw her baby into a fire, it's hard to get too exercised about what party someone belongs to.

Jeane Kirkpatrick said the experience of being the U.S. ambassador to the UN left her "in every way a sadder and wiser woman about the world." This is one of the rare times when I disagree with her. My experience hasn't left me sad; it's left me more grateful than ever to be an American. Not complacent. Not convinced of our superiority. But *grateful* for all the tools we have that allow us to become a better nation. Our ability to speak freely, to debate, to worship, and to determine our own destinies—these are things to be grateful for, and to preserve. At the United Nations I worked every day alongside people whose governments denied these things.

I'm not blind to America's faults. I am the daughter of Indian immigrants, born in a small town in rural South Carolina. I was born a brown girl in a black-and-white world. My sister and I— just four and eight years old—were disqualified from a children's pageant because we weren't white or black. We were somewhere in between. The pageant organizers thought in categories, and they didn't have a category for us.

We were the only Indian American family in my hometown of Bamberg, probably the first Indian Americans most people there had ever seen. My father wore a turban, as he does to this day. We were outsiders. We stood out. I remember the stares. And I remember when the stares became whispers, and the whispers became fear, and that fear showed itself in suspicion and exclusion.

My heart hurts when I think about the way people would look at my dad in his turban, so he put an American flag sticker on his car, as so many other Sikhs did after September 11, 2001. Once when I was young, my family went to a picnic at a local country club. It hurts even now to remember how no one would sit next to us or even acknowledge us, so we ate and we left.

And when I ran for governor, the pain was bipartisan. An African American Democrat denounced me as not a "real minority" but "a conservative with a tan." And a white Republican called me a "raghead."

This kind of pain stays with you, and it can overwhelm you if you let it. Many different kinds of Americans endure this pain. I've tried to use my own, not for blame, but for knowledge. I've used my experiences to acknowledge the pain of others and to work to make sure no one else feels it. But I have refused to let it define me. Pain is real. Victimhood is a choice.

My story is an American story. It couldn't have been written anywhere else. Yes, we were outsiders when I was growing up. But that's not unusual. People who are different are outsiders everywhere in the world. America is different because our community came to accept us. Our country gave us the opportunity to strive and succeed. It gave my dad the opportunity to teach at a college. It gave my mom the opportunity to open a business. And it gave me the opportunity to become governor and then UN ambassador. That's America.

My story is also a South Carolinian story. I am so proud of my state. While I was governor, South Carolina continued to grow and prosper and defy the worst stereotypes about us. We attracted over $20 billion in new capital investment. We had the fastest-growing exports of any southeastern state. Trade groups nicknamed us the "Beast of the Southeast." And as a result we had record low unemployment.

We elected the first African American senator in our state's history, and the first African American senator from the South since Reconstruction, my friend Senator Tim Scott. And after the nation watched in horror as a white South Carolinian police officer shot a fleeing black man named Walter Scott in the back, we didn't riot. We became the first state in the Union to require every police officer to wear a body camera.

After so long being a place where people saw racial hatred and discrimination, South Carolina was becoming a place people could look to for racial harmony and acceptance. It was a growing, thriving place with people of many different colors and backgrounds, living respectfully as neighbors and fellow citizens. Life was good and I was proud.

Then an avowed racist opened fire in a Charleston church. Nine African American worshippers were murdered. It shattered my world.

1

The Murders in Charleston

I've never said the Charleston killer's name out loud. I physically can't without feeling sick. I refer to him only as "the shooter" or "the killer." I don't want him to have a name. He doesn't deserve to have a single American know about him because of the lives he took and the pain he inflicted on my state. He is nothing but a reminder that real hate exists in the world.

I saw the true face of evil in the man who killed nine worshippers in that Charleston church on June 17, 2015. I wouldn't wish the memory of him on my worst enemies. I can't imagine how it torments the families of the victims. I know it's never left me. When the killer was apprehended in North Carolina after fleeing Charleston, I directed our law enforcement officials to use the plane I used as governor to get him to South Carolina as fast as possible. Our state law enforcement director, Chief Mark Keel, asked if I was sure I wanted to do that. I soon understood why. I watched in horror as television news broadcast the killer getting on the plane and sitting in the seat I usually sat in. Whenever I rode in the plane after that, I was disgusted. All I could think about was that I was sitting in the same seat as the killer—someone with more hate in his heart than I could comprehend.

I first learned about the shooting when I was getting the kids ready for bed in the governor's mansion in Columbia. It came in a text from my chief of staff, James Burns. As governor, I had a real love-hate relationship with my phone. It kept me in constant touch with my staff and other state officials. But whenever it went off at night I got a bad feeling in the pit of my stomach. Over the years there had been way too many calls with bad news. I learned about prison riots in which officers were attacked and held hostage by the inmates, about school shootings, a state agency director having a stroke, the deaths of soldiers and state employees, and hurricanes bearing down on South Carolina—all from late-night calls or texts on my phone.

That night, James's text didn't have much information. But a few minutes later, a call came in from Chief Keel. He was a man of few words in any circumstance. That night, he got straight to the point.

"Governor, there has been a shooting at Mother Emanuel Church. We believe there could be casualties. It doesn't look good," he said.

Mother Emanuel is the name South Carolinians have for the Emanuel African Methodist Episcopal (AME) Church. It is a fixture of Charleston and the oldest AME church in the South. It was also the church in which a beloved state senator, Clementa Pinckney, was a senior pastor.

Senator Pinckney was a Democrat from a rural area in Jasper County. He was a tall man with a great, deep voice. He had been elected to the state legislature when he was quite young and had served with genuine concern for the people of South Carolina. He and I had shared a stage just weeks before to announce new jobs created in his district. He was gracious and appreciative. His smile had a way of making you feel calm.

Chief Keel was already headed to Charleston. I asked him to be in touch with me as soon as he arrived. And then, without thinking, I called Senator Pinckney. I got his voice mail.

"Senator, I wanted to call and let you know that I just heard about the shooting at Mother Emanuel," I said. "The chief and I are on it. He is headed to Charleston now. Please know whatever your congregation or the families need, we will be in full force to assist. I'm so very sorry. Please give me a call back when you receive this."

It never for a second occurred to me that Senator Pinckney would be at the church that evening. It was a Wednesday night. The legislature was in session in Columbia, a full two-hour drive from Charleston. But as I waited for him to call me back, the horrific dimensions of the shooting began to take shape. Each text and each call were one more kick in the gut. By the early morning hours of June 18, 2015, it was clear that South Carolina had experienced an unspeakable tragedy. Chief Keel called to tell me that there had been eight casualties at the church. Another person had died at the hospital, for a total of nine murdered. The shooter was still at large, he said. And Senator Pinckney was among the casualties.

Of all the terrible memories I have from the Mother Emanuel tragedy, learning that night that Senator Pinckney was never going to call me back is among the worst. The fact that his phone was ringing in his pocket as he lay on the floor of his church will haunt me for the rest of my life.

By dawn, I was getting ready to leave for Charleston. The kids were still asleep. But I didn't want them to hear about the shooting from someone else. So I went to their rooms and began one of the most difficult conversations I've ever had with them. I told them I had to go to Charleston and I would probably not be home that night.

"There was a shooting in a church," I said. My thirteen-year-old son Nalin asked me, "Mom, why would someone shoot in a church?" His older sister Rena asked the same thing. It broke my heart to hear this question. Church was supposed to be a safe place. All I could do was assure them we would catch the person who did it.

"Everything will be okay," I said. "But I need to be there to make sure it happens."

IT WAS STILL VERY EARLY when I arrived in Charleston. I immediately went to the command center the police had set up near the crime scene. There was an eerie quiet on the streets around the church. The police had cordoned off the area so members of the media and onlookers couldn't get near the crime scene. Officers who had worked through the night were still working, carefully marking the spots where the seventy-four shell casings the killer left behind had fallen.

The police had reviewed the security cameras outside the church and had some good news. They had clear images of a young white man with a bowl haircut entering the church the night before at 8:17 p.m. and then exiting, gun in hand, at 9:07 p.m. Chief Keel told me the police believed they knew who he was. They had spoken to his family members about where he might have gone.

"Chief, tell me he has a mental illness," I said. I couldn't understand how a sane person could have done this. I didn't *want* to understand how a person in their right mind was capable of such evil. But the chief said no. From talking with his family, he learned there had been no sign of mental illness.

"We believe this is a hate crime," Chief Keel said.

There was a press conference scheduled for 11:00 a.m. I was in the car on my way there when I got a call. Someone had spotted the killer in North Carolina, and he was in custody. For the first time, I felt like I could breathe. I needed him back in South Carolina as soon as possible to be charged. It was then that I told Chief Keel to use the state plane.

The plan was for Charleston police chief Greg Mullen to lead off the press conference with the announcement of the apprehension of the killer. Then Charleston mayor Joe Riley would speak, and then me. I knew I had to focus on what I could possibly say to give strength to my fellow South Carolinians. I needed to be calm. I needed to assure the people they were safe. But all I could think about was that South Carolina would never be the same. Everyone's sense of safety—even in church—had been violated. People would constantly be looking over their shoulders, constantly expecting the worst.

I needed to be a source of calm and strength in a state that was grieving, but I didn't know if I could be. I called my friend and advisor, Jon Lerner, from the car.

"This will bring the state to her knees. I'm so upset at that thought," I told him. "I'm worried about being strong enough and knowing what to say to the people." Jon's advice was wise and assuring, as usual. He said it was a time to not hold back, to be straightforward and completely honest with the people of South Carolina. They would understand if I lost my composure. They were all feeling the same way.

The summer heat was almost unbearable as we gathered before the media. When it came time for me to speak, I thanked the mayor for his leadership and I thanked law enforcement for apprehending the shooter so quickly. And then I began to address the people of South Carolina. As I started to speak, all the anxiety, the sadness, and the anger I had been bottling up for the past twelve hours came rushing to the surface.

"We woke up today . . ." I began. And then I lost it. As I continued, my voice cracked and my eyes welled up with tears: ". . . and the heart and soul of South Carolina was broken."

My mind went back to my conversation with my children just hours before. I talked about how all South Carolina's parents were forced to have that same conversation with their kids today. I thanked the American people for the outpouring of love and concern we had already received. I asked the people of South Carolina to come together and be strong. The families of the victims needed our love and our prayers, I said. We can get through this together.

When the press conference was finished, I was angry and disappointed with myself. I had done what I was afraid I would do. I had lost control of my emotions. As a woman, this is something that I have always been particularly sensitive to. And at this time of all times, when the people of my state needed strength and reassurance, I felt like I had showed them weakness.

My press aides had been watching while I spoke. I looked at them and said, "I am so mad at myself. Why did I cry?" Their response was one that I needed to hear, not only that day, but in the days and weeks that followed. You're only human, they told me through their own tears. Anyone would have the same reaction. And they were right. South Carolinians needed to grieve, and I was one of them, too.

After the press conference we went to a prayer vigil. Hundreds gathered inside Morris Brown AME Church, just blocks away from Mother Emmanuel. Hundreds more crowded the streets outside. There were South Carolinians of all colors and faiths. There were tears. There was anger. But most of all, an enormous, palpable pain filled the church. Again, I felt the need to protect my state and its people.

"What happened in that church last night is not South Carolina," I told the crowd of mourners. "What's happening today in this church—these are the people of South Carolina."

WHILE WE WERE GRIEVING IN Charleston, 243 miles to the northwest in Shelby, North Carolina, the killer was confessing the details of his crime. Later, Chief Keel filled me in on his interrogation by two FBI agents. He said the killer was calm and relaxed. The shooter chuckled at times as he described how he wanted to kill black people—lots of them. He explained that he researched African American churches to find a place where large numbers of black people gathered.

The Charleston killings were planned and premeditated. The shooter chose Mother Emanuel because it was the oldest black church in the South. He went there before the shooting and asked a woman exiting the church what times the services were held. She told him there was Bible study on Wednesday nights.

The Wednesday night of the murders, the killer entered through the front door of the church. When he walked in, there were twelve people singing and reciting verses. They saw him. He didn't look like them. He didn't act like them. But they didn't throw him out or call the police. Instead they pulled up a chair and prayed with him for almost an hour. The killer later acknowledged how nice they were to him. For a split second, he had second thoughts about doing what he had come there to do. But his hate overcame him. In his demented mind, blacks were hurting white people and someone had to do something. He said that over and over during his interrogation: Someone had to do something. So as the Mother Emanuel worshippers closed their eyes for their final prayer, the killer pulled out a semiautomatic pistol and began shooting. He went through seven magazines of bullets. He had an eighth, which he said he was saving to shoot himself with when the police showed up. But when the killing was over and he opened the door of the church, there were no police. Inside, there were eleven people shot on the floor, eight of whom were already dead.

Even before any of these horrific details were known to anyone outside law enforcement, the shootings became breaking national news. Media began to pour into Charleston. Within thirty-six hours of the event, the streets surrounding Mother Emanuel had been completely taken over by the press. There were tents, cameras, and communications equipment extending as far as the eye could see around the church. All the local media were there, in addition to the national broadcast and cable networks, as well as international news organizations.

With the national and international media came a different perspective on the killings. I was doing everything I could to keep the focus on the families of the victims. South Carolina needed time to process what had happened. But many in the national and international media wanted sensationalism. They wanted to take our tragedy and use it to score political or cultural points. Before all the names of the victims were even known, mostly out-of-state voices were raising issues like the death penalty, gun control, and whether South Carolina had really left its history of racial animus behind.

President Barack Obama spoke to the nation the morning after the killings. He looked tired and defeated. He and Michelle had known Senator Pinckney and other members of the church. It was clear that he was feeling the same kind of pain that we were feeling in South Carolina. But toward the end of his remarks, President Obama made a historical analogy that I thought was wrong. He mentioned the four little African American girls who were killed in a church bombing in Birmingham, Alabama, in 1963. Their deaths had shocked the conscience of the nation and been a significant motivator to the civil rights movement. President Obama quoted Dr. Martin Luther King, Jr., who said of the 1963 victims, "We must be concerned not merely about who murdered them, but about the system, *the way of life,* the philosophy which produced the murderers" (emphasis mine).

I felt even more strongly than the president about the need for understanding exactly why the killer took the lives of nine people in a Charleston Church. I wanted justice for the victims and to make sure something like this never happened again in my state. But I also knew a lot had changed in the South since 1963.

I GREW UP IN RURAL South Carolina. I was born in a town called Bamberg, which had a population of just twenty-five hundred when my parents moved there in 1969. Mom and Dad left behind lives of relative privilege in India to come to America. Mom grew up surrounded by servants in a six-story house in Punjab. My father's father was a commanding officer in a horse-mounted regiment of the British colonial army. Not only did my parents leave behind comfort and privilege when they left India, they left behind everyone and almost everything they had ever known.

They came to the United States because they knew it would be a place of opportunity for their children. They reminded us every day how blessed we were to live in America. And it was true. America would show my family discrimination and challenges, but it would also show us acceptance and opportunity.

My parents are proud of their heritage. They didn't leave that behind when they came to Bamberg. So we dealt with it the only way we knew how. We stuck together. We worked hard. We tried to fit in.

Like so many immigrant families, we didn't know what we didn't have. Mom and Dad worked all the time, so we kids had to take care of each other. I had a happy childhood, but I learned early on that the ways in which I was different—my religion, my race, and even my gender—would be a constant in my life. They weren't going to go away. So I did what my parents had always taught us to do: I focused on finding similarities with other children and avoiding the things that separated us. I still remember their words: "Your job is not to show people how you are different. Your job is to show them how you are similar."

But the culture in South Carolina at the time made this difficult. People were categorized by the color of their skin, and it affected the way we saw each other. I remember one day in third grade coming out at recess to play kickball with the other kids. When I walked onto the playground, the kids were all huddled together and staring at me. I noticed that they were separated into a black group and a white group. I got a familiar, sick feeling in the pit of my stomach. "Are we playing today?" I said. A girl responded, "We are. You're not." When I asked why, she replied, "You can play with us, but you have to pick a side. Are you white or are you black?" I panicked for a moment. Then I did what I was rapidly growing used to doing: I changed the subject. I grabbed the ball and ran toward the field. "I'm neither!" I yelled. "I'm brown!"

Before long, we were all playing kickball.

There were other times, however, when changing the subject wasn't possible. One of the stories the media liked most to repeat about me when I was running for governor was the story of the Wee Miss Bamberg Pageant. The media liked it because it confirmed many of their preconceived notions of the South, particularly rural South Carolina. But I sometimes tell this story for another reason: to demonstrate the damage that we do when we put our differences— instead of our similarities—at the center of our identity.

We weren't a pageant family, but the big thing to do in Bamberg was to enter your daughters in the Wee Miss Bamberg Pageant. My mother entered my sister, Simmi, and me in the pageant when we were four and eight years old. I wore a ruffly white dress and sang "This Land Is Your Land." After all the little girls had performed, the organizers lined us up on the stage. The little white girls were on one side, and the little black girls were on the other. In the middle were Simmi and me.

The pageant traditionally had two winners, a black winner and a white winner. But the organizers didn't know what to do with us. They called us out of line and said, "We don't have a place for you." Then they sent us home with consolation prizes. I got a beach ball. It was only later when I realized what had happened. I don't think the organizers of the pageant were bad people. The judges didn't want to make either race mad by putting us in their category. It was easier to just disqualify us. They were operating under a bad set of rules that perpetuated racial prejudice, even if it was a soft kind of prejudice.

There were other painful memories. My parents told us about how no one would rent them a house when they first came to Bamberg. They were clearly foreigners. Plus, the word had gotten around that my father worked at the "black school." He had found a job as a professor of biology at Voorhees College, a historically black college in nearby Denmark, South Carolina. When my parents finally found a house, the seller said they had to buy it, not rent it. And he had conditions. They couldn't entertain black people in it. And they had to sell it back to him when they wanted to move.

These were painful experiences for my parents. I learned important lessons from them. The pain of being an outsider—of being judged unfairly—never really leaves you. But it gives you an appreciation for the different experiences of different groups, even in a place as open and accepting as America. More important, it allows you to see and to appreciate how much has changed.

When I was about ten, I went on a trip with my father to Columbia. This was a treat. Columbia was the "big city," and it was precious time for me to spend alone with my dad. On the way, we stopped by a fruit and vegetable stand on the roadside. There are great ones in South Carolina, and my parents loved buying fruit and vegetables directly from a farm whenever they could.

We had the place to ourselves. No other customers were there, just the owners. After we had shopped for a few minutes, two police cars suddenly came charging up to the market. The officers got out of their cars and approached the owners of the stand by the cash register. As they talked, I noticed they were looking at my father and me. Then I realized that the police were there *because* of us. My father just kept picking out fruit like nothing was happening. And when he was done shopping, he went up to the register, said hello to the owners, and paid for his produce.

We got back in the car in silence. My heart ached for my father. Even then, I knew this was something he experienced often. He hoped I hadn't noticed but I did. We didn't speak a word to each other the entire way home.

This experience was a painful and inescapable fact of my childhood. I used to pass that same fruit stand traveling in and out of Columbia when I was an adult and in government. Each time, I remembered my father's pain and embarrassment. But more important, I realized that the same thing would never happen today. South Carolina is a different place. My story is proof of that.

My family had felt the sting of ethnic and racial discrimination. But we'd also seen the South change. The same town that rejected me from a pageant accepted me into a Girl Scout troop, an experience that changed my life. People in the town helped my dad get a job at a community college. They shopped at my mother's small business. My home state isn't perfect—no place is. But it is a place where neighbors help neighbors. My home state is a place of faith, values, and patriotism.

SO I THOUGHT PRESIDENT OBAMA was wrong after the Mother Emanuel murders when he implied that the South was somehow to blame. I didn't believe then and I don't believe now that our "way of life" or our "system" created the killer. I would not have been elected governor if South Carolina were a racially intolerant place. Tim Scott would not have been elected senator if South Carolina was consumed with racial hatred.

Later, on the day of the murders, the president called me from

Air Force One. I had met and spoken with President Obama many times. We had always had what I thought was a cordial relationship. So I was glad to hear from him. When a governor goes through a crisis, you look to your president for support. You look to your president for understanding and partnership.

From the moment he got on the phone, the president was very short and to the point. There was a coldness in his voice. The president said he was calling about the shooting, but he didn't offer his condolences. When I told him I was worried about South Carolinians being able to get through the tragedy without violence, he didn't offer any help or words of encouragement. He seemed to feel the way he had hinted at before—that South Carolinians were partly to blame for the murders. When I hung up the phone, it didn't feel like we had had a conversation. It felt like President Obama was going through the motions, checking a box. It seemed to me like South Carolina was going to have to go at it alone.

As the details of the shooter's racist motives became known, the finger-pointing increased. And as the theories about how South Carolina had somehow produced this monster multiplied, my instinct to protect my people grew. I made time the Friday after the shooting to appear on some national news programs to talk about the murders. After a couple questions about the condition of the victims' families, these interviews always ·turned to questions of guns, race, and the South. It was clear to me how strong a hold the worst stereotypes about the South had on some in the media. It was as if they, too, believed nothing had changed since 1963. I knew it was my job to push back, and I did.

On *CBS This Morning* Gayle King asked me if the shootings were a sign there needed to be "a conversation" about race in South Carolina. Her implication was clear: Wasn't it time for South

Carolinians to admit that they are still intolerant—or worse—
of racial minorities? I replied that South Carolinians had already
started a conversation about race. It had begun two months earlier
when a white police officer shot a black man named Walter Scott
in the back as Scott was running away from him. The incident was
captured on video, and the whole country had seen it.

This was at a time when racial incidents were causing riots
and destruction in places like Ferguson, Missouri, and Baltimore,
Maryland. South Carolinians were horrified by what they saw, I
told Gayle. But we didn't react with riots. We started a conversation about police accountability and safety. We came together and
changed the law: We passed the most thorough police body-camera
law in the nation. We became the first state to require all police
departments to have their officers wear body cameras.

What I wanted to say to Gayle King, but I didn't, was that
South Carolina was becoming a model for how to deal with difficult racial issues without violence and division. We were confronting police misconduct, poverty, and unemployment with respectful
debate and constructive measures. So much of what the media and
some others said and did in the aftermath of the Mother Emanuel
Church shootings seemed designed to divide people. But what the
people needed most was to be united in our grief. We needed to
stay focused on the families of the victims and on healing. The
policy debates about what else we could do differently in the future
would come. We would have those conversations and we would act.
But we would do it our way. And for now, we weren't taking the
national media's bait.

"I understand what y'all want," I told Gayle King. "But the
people of South Carolina need to heal. There will be policy discus-

sions, and you will hear me come out and talk about it. But right now, I'm not doing that to the people of my state."

Just over twenty-four hours after I said these words, the killer's website would be discovered. It featured his manifesto of racial hatred. Alongside his hateful words were photos of the killer posing with the Confederate flag. I knew then that the reckoning I had hoped to forestall for my state, if only for a few weeks, would be coming sooner than I had hoped.

2

The Flag Comes Down

I went to every one of the funerals. Most were held in Mother Emanuel Church. Every funeral included an open casket. I watched family members fall over their loved ones' bodies in complete despair. I heard them cry out, asking God why. Every family asked me to speak. Sometimes I would hold it together. Sometimes I would break down. I tried to honor the dead and comfort the living. But in the end, I couldn't do much to diminish the pain. It destroyed me to watch the people I was supposed to be taking care of suffer so much.

Every funeral was special, in its own way. The pastor would preach at the top of his lungs, sometimes with tears running down his cheeks. We sang as if we were trying to sing the sadness away. I would stare at the face of the deceased on the program as family members told stories about his or her amazing life and deep faith. Listening allowed me to meet each of the individuals who would come to be called part of the "Emanuel Nine." I learned about the difference they made in their time on earth, in their families, their church, and their communities. Each night, I took the program home and introduced the person I had met that day to my children.

There was Senator Pinckney, the lead pastor of Mother Emanuel. I had wondered, when I heard he was one of the casualties, why he had gone all the way to Charleston on a Wednesday night during the legislative session. I learned that he had gone because they were certifying new members to preach at the church that day, and he wanted to be there.

DePayne Middleton was one of those new preachers. She left four daughters, and she had the voice of an angel.

Daniel Simmons was a veteran who had dedicated his life to service. After he served his country, he worked with other veterans and helped people with disabilities find jobs.

Sharonda Singleton was a teacher and a track coach. She was a mom to every one of her students. But the best tribute to Sharonda is her own three children. They are a living testament to who she was as a mother and as a person.

Tywanza Sanders was the youngest victim. He had just finished college, and the world was his oyster. On the night of the murders, Tywanza stood in front of his eighty-seven-year-old great-aunt, Suzie, and told the killer, "You don't have to do this. We mean no harm to you." Suzie Jackson died along with Tywanza. She was devoted to her family and never had an unkind word to say about anyone. She was known to take into her home people who needed a place to stay.

Ethel Lance had a sweet smile, but it was hard for her to hold. She had lost her daughter to breast cancer a couple of years earlier. Her heart was broken, but she was known to sing, "One day at a time, sweet Jesus, that's all I ask of you. Give me the strength every day to do what I have to do."

Myra Thompson had also been certified to preach that night. She had spent weeks preparing to teach her first Bible study class on the night of the murders.

And there was Cynthia Hurd. She was a librarian. They named a local library in her honor after the tragedy. She had grown up in Mother Emanuel Church. So it is not surprising that her life motto was, "Be kinder than necessary."

Going to these nine funerals was the hardest thing I've ever had to do in my life. But my pain couldn't begin to match the pain of the families and friends I was surrounded by. The families were so broken but their grace in the face of such hate and such tragedy was awe-inspiring. Each kind gesture, each act of forgiveness, deepened my resolve to not let division take over South Carolina. It was my role to protect these people, to find a way for them to heal. I felt this responsibility acutely.

On the Saturday after the murders, the killer's ramblings were found online. My press people showed me the website, and I knew instantly that the national media was going to do all it could to brand my state with its hateful contents. Interspersed with a twenty-five-hundred-word racist manifesto were pictures of the killer with the Confederate flag. Alongside rants about the inferiority of African Americans was a picture of the killer on his haunches, waving the flag. One showed him looking menacingly at the camera with the flag in one hand and a gun in the other. Other pictures showed him burning and spitting on the American flag.

THE DISCOVERY OF THE KILLER'S website made my job keeping South Carolina from ripping itself apart immensely more difficult. The Confederate flag had divided South Carolinians and riled outsiders for as long as I could remember. For many good-hearted people of my state, the flag was a symbol of heritage and ancestry. For others, it was a symbol of hate and oppression. I could understand both points of view. I also knew one would have to give way to the other.

My approach had always been that displaying the flag was a matter for South Carolinians to decide. In 1996, then governor David Beasley, a Republican, called for the removal of the Confederate flag from where it then flew atop the statehouse dome. The fight that followed paralyzed the state legislature for weeks. It was vicious and relationship-ending. It was also career-ending. The proposal failed, but the fact that Governor Beasley had proposed it contributed significantly to his reelection defeat in 1998. Then, in 2000, a compromise was reached—sort of. The flag was moved from the top of the statehouse to a Confederate monument on the statehouse grounds. It no longer flew at the top of our capitol, but it was still in a prominent place, and still on the capitol grounds.

When I became governor, the Confederate flag was a defining issue for how a lot of Americans regarded South Carolina. I made a point, early on, of talking to both Republicans and Democrats to see if there was the political will to take the flag down once and for all. Members from both parties pushed back against the idea. Those who had been in office for the 1996 Beasley attempt were particularly vocal in opposition. It had been so contentious. Members had received death threats. Even many African American Democrats were privately opposed to the idea of reopening the flag debate.

But the images of the Charleston killer with the Confederate flag changed all that. A flag is unlike other symbols. Monuments represent a point in time. They are unmoving. A flag waves. It represents something living and breathing about a place and a people.

The Mother Emanuel shooter had made sure that anyone who saw the Confederate flag would now think of the killer and the image of him holding it. The evil act he had committed had robbed the good-intentioned South Carolinians who supported the flag of this symbol of heritage and service. He had encouraged everyone's worst stereotype for our state. Clearly, something had to be done. But at the same time, I worried that allowing the killer to define what the flag represented for everyone was a surrender. Why should he, of all people, be given that power?

I was exhausted, physically and mentally. My husband Michael had been away for two weeks for military training with the South Carolina Army National Guard. I missed him always, but in the aftermath of the shooting, I felt his absence more than usual. Michael has always been my most trusted advisor. He always knows how to talk me through a problem and get to the right solution. I get so much comfort and strength from him. I needed that comfort and strength when I returned to the governor's residence in Columbia the Friday after the shooting. Michael was also returning that evening. I texted him on my way home:

> I need to talk to you when we get home. I've got some things in my head, and I just need to know if I'm thinking right.

The next day, when the pictures of the killer with the Confederate flag were discovered, I felt panic creeping up on me. I knew, more surely than before, that what was to come would not be good. My thoughts were racing when Michael and I sat down to talk. How could we keep South Carolinians together and help each other heal? How could we withstand the onslaught of the national media? How could we avoid racial violence? I was deeply conflicted

for my state, but I think I already knew what I was going to decide.
And for the first time, I found myself saying it out loud.

"I don't see any way that the flag can continue to fly at the statehouse," I told Michael.

He immediately agreed. We had a long conversation about how
the flag represented evil to so many South Carolinians. It shouldn't
fly at the capitol. At the same time, we couldn't allow the incident
to result in a ban on displaying the flag altogether. Anyone should
have the right to fly it on their own property if he or she wanted to.
We talked about putting the flag from the statehouse in a museum.
Michael helped me think through all the things we needed to do to
avoid violence and allow the state to heal.

We needed to plan carefully on how to deal with the legislature.
History had shown that calling for the flag to come down would
almost certainly cause massive debate and division in South Carolina. The easier thing to do would be to avoid a decision, to call for
a commission to study the matter. But it was past time that my state
confront this issue once and for all. The flag was holding us back.
South Carolina was moving forward as a place of opportunity and
prosperity in the New South. We couldn't continue to do so with
the flag literally hanging over us. Besides, I told Michael, I would
never be able to look our children in the eye and tell them the
flag was still flying on the statehouse grounds. Not after Mother
Emanuel. Not after what I'd seen.

The next day, a Sunday, I called my senior staff to the residence
to tell them about my decision. As governor, I couldn't remove the
flag on my own. Decades earlier, the legislature had passed a law
requiring a two-thirds majority of both houses to take it down. The
current legislative session was over, but lawmakers would return
the coming Tuesday to finish working on the budget. That meant

that the announcement had to be the next day, on Monday. I knew
from the 1996 experience that getting a two-thirds vote was going
to be a heavy lift. We had to act fast.

I didn't want to surprise anyone, so we set up a series of face-to-
face meetings with the Republican and Democratic leadership in
the state legislature. I also called in the congressional delegation. I
delivered the same message at each of the meetings: I was going to
hold a press conference at 4:00 p.m. to call for removing the Confederate flag from the statehouse grounds. I told my colleagues that
if they chose to stand with me, I would be forever grateful. If they
decided not to join me, I said, I would never let anyone know we
had discussed it. To this day, I have kept that promise.

There were some surprises among the reactions to my call for
removing the flag. Many of the people you would think would
support it didn't. And many you would think would object were
for it. Overwhelmingly, those who disagreed with removing the
flag argued that it would be too divisive. They were angry that I
would even raise the issue. It would cause a race war, and that was
the last thing we needed at that point, they said. I argued just the
opposite—that this was the healing gesture that we desperately
needed. South Carolinians who want to fly the Confederate flag
would still be able to on their own property. But it would no longer
fly as a banner for all South Carolinians on the statehouse grounds.
I urged my colleagues to seize this opportunity to respectfully move
the flag to a museum and finally end this debate.

As the members left my office, it was impossible for me to read
what they were thinking. I had taken a huge gamble. I was worried
that no one would stand with me at the press conference. Michael
had been with me during the meetings, and I knew he would be
by my side. That was an unbelievable reassurance. But I hoped and

prayed we wouldn't be alone when the cameras and the reporters showed up.

I held my breath and I prayed. Then, just before the press conference was to begin, lawmakers began to show up. I exhaled. Democratic congressman Jim Clyburn was there. Charleston mayor Joe Riley and House minority leader Todd Rutherford also came. Even though some had expressed misgivings about moving the flag, the Republican members of the South Carolina congressional delegation showed up. Amazingly, Republican state senator John Courson, who had a wall of his office dedicated to Confederate general Robert E. Lee, showed up. With him was state senator Paul Thurmond, the son of the one-time segregationist leader and South Carolina legend Strom Thurmond.

Governor Beasley was also there. A few hours earlier he had shown up in my office. I hadn't seen him since my inauguration. I said, "Governor, you started this." And he answered, "But, Governor, you need to finish it."

Governor Beasley stood next to me for the duration of the press conference.

I was proud to have a bipartisan group with me. It was critical that moving the flag not just be my cause. It had to be the cause of the people of South Carolina.

"We are not going to allow this symbol to divide us any longer," I said. "The fact that it causes so much pain is enough to move it from the capitol grounds. It is, after all, a capitol that belongs to all of us."

IT WAS A MOMENT OF unity for our state, and I said so. But it was just the beginning. There was still a long road ahead. The flag was an issue that cut deep. We had to pull off a delicate balancing act. I didn't want to overplay my hand with the legislature. Many members looked on the Confederate flag with reverence. It was a symbol of their ancestors who had died and a heritage that they felt was under siege by Washington, Hollywood, and the national media. I couldn't simply strong-arm these legislators into changing their minds, and I wouldn't. I had to appeal to their compassion and their patriotism. I had to convince them that this was the best decision we could make for the state we all loved.

Further complicating the situation was the fact that South Carolina at the time was crawling with candidates for the Republican presidential nomination. It was June 2015, and our primary wouldn't take place until February of the next year. But South Carolina was a critical early voting state. We had predicted the GOP nominee in every presidential election except one since 1980. With so much on the line, the huge Republican field of candidates was already campaigning hard in the state. The last thing we needed was for the flag issue to once again become embroiled in presidential politics.

South Carolinians deserved the right to make the decision about the flag for ourselves. So I got on the phone with most of the presidential candidates to ask them not to comment on the flag issue. My message was simple: Do me a favor and let me handle this. To their credit, some, like Wisconsin governor Scott Walker and Louisiana governor Bobby Jindal, called me before I could call them. They asked me what they could do to help. I appreciated those gestures more than I could say.

In the end, all the candidates honored our request not to comment—that is, until a former presidential nominee, Mitt Romney, reopened the wound with a statement a few days after the shooting. In a tweet, Governor Romney called the flag a "symbol of racial hatred" and called for its removal from the capitol in order to honor the Charleston victims. President Obama tweeted, "Good point, Mitt."

I respected the moral sense that led both these men to make their positions clear. But they were making my job harder. That day I called Mitt and lit into him. I am trying to hold a state together, I said, and this isn't helping. He had been a governor, he should know that.

Mitt said he felt compelled to speak out against the flag because he hadn't been forceful enough in his 2012 run. I told him the situation was not about him. Less than a year earlier, riots had broken out on the streets of Ferguson, Missouri, following the shooting of a black teenager by police. Just months earlier, Baltimore had erupted in violence following the arrest of an African American, Freddie Gray, who died in police custody. There were groups on both sides of these incidents who were now threatening to bring their protests to South Carolina. I didn't want my state to become another Ferguson. Mitt's comments might have made him feel better, but they decreased the chances of South Carolina coming through this crisis in one piece.

Still, the statement had already had its effect. It forced each of the Republican candidates to put out statements of their own on the flag. Thankfully, they all made it clear that whether it remained on the statehouse grounds was an issue that should ultimately be decided by the people of South Carolina.

Even before the candidates and ex-candidates weighed in, the tension in the state had been building. As soon as I announced my decision, South Carolina became a target for outsiders and extremists. The Ku Klux Klan and the New Black Panthers announced

rallies in Charleston. My office received approximately ten thousand emails in the days following the announcement. Some urged
that the flag be brought down. Some said it wasn't a symbol of
hate but of heritage. A frightening number contained death threats.
Legislators debating the flying of the flag also received threats on
their lives. An activist from North Carolina climbed the thirty-foot
flagpole and successfully removed the flag before she was stopped
by security.

LOOKING BACK, IT WAS A kind of blessing that the flag debate
occurred after South Carolina had weathered the police shooting
of Walter Scott, just months before. My family was on vacation
for spring break when I got the call from state law enforcement
that Scott had been killed by a police officer in North Charleston.
Almost instantly, the video was everywhere. We watched over and
over as Scott was shot in the back as he ran away from a policeman.
All I could think of was his family. How terrible it must be to watch
your son or your brother get killed nonstop on cable news.

The Walter Scott shooting had all the same race and law enforcement elements of the Ferguson and Baltimore shootings. A white
cop. An unarmed black victim. Video evidence of the crime. Those
earlier shootings had already sent too many Americans to their political corners. They had pitted blacks against whites, and citizens
against law enforcement. The Scott shooting had the potential to
stir the same ugly emotions of Ferguson and Baltimore, times two.
My goal was to do everything I could to avoid this happening in
South Carolina. If things got ugly, there would be little chance that
Walter Scott's death would result in any change. I talked with my
staff, legislators, and law enforcement leaders, trying to figure out

how we could defuse the situation in a way that would keep the police accountable and see justice for the Scott family.

We knew we had to act fast, before the situation deteriorated. It was inevitable that much of the media would rush to paint South Carolina as a racist southern state full of bad cops. But I knew South Carolina law enforcement. The vast majority of our police officers were fair and dedicated public servants. The officer who killed Walter Scott was a tragic exception. Still, we weren't going to overlook his actions.

We began immediately to push the legislature to pass a bill requiring all police in the state to wear body cameras. It was going to call for some careful negotiating. The same divisions over race and law enforcement that were hardening in other parts of the country were also present in our legislature. We argued that our body-camera bill was a win-win for both sides. It gave victims of police misconduct the evidence they needed, and it protected police from false or frivolous claims of abuse.

When I signed the body-camera bill in front of the Felix C. Davis Community Center in North Charleston, I found myself once again immensely proud of my fellow South Carolinians. We had passed the first statewide law in the country mandating police body cameras, and we did so with the support of victims' rights groups and law enforcement. Most important, as I signed the bill, Walter Scott's family was there by my side. We had created something good and necessary out of the terrible tragedy they had suffered. The people of South Carolina had set an example for the nation.

THE SCOTT FAMILY WAS IN the back of my mind when I vowed that politics would not intrude on the funerals of the Emanuel

Nine—at least not if I could help it. The memorial services were for the families and their loved ones. The funerals presented neither the time nor the place for political statements.

Both the Reverend Jesse Jackson and the Reverend Al Sharpton came to Charleston shortly after the shootings. They were both present, along with Senator Scott, Mayor Riley, myself, and others, at the first of the funerals, for Ethel Lance. Sharpton's presence was more than a little unnerving. The family of Walter Scott had asked Sharpton to stay away from Walter's funeral months earlier. A source close to the family told the media that they didn't want a "Ferguson-type circus" at the funeral.

It was an emotionally wrenching ceremony. Five of Ethel's seven beautiful grandchildren came up to the pulpit and one by one praised their grandmother's love and generosity. But when Al Sharpton spoke, for some reason he took a shot at me. He said he'd never met me. He said he had led a protest outside the statehouse and I hadn't come out to speak with him.

I couldn't imagine what he was talking about and why he was talking about it now, at a funeral. When it was my turn to speak, I described Ethel and her children and grandchildren. She had never finished high school but she had made sure they all went to college. She was an amazing woman. And before I finished, I had to address Al Sharpton's comment.

"Reverend Sharpton, I want to say this to you," I said from the pulpit. "If you had been standing outside of my office protesting, if you had taken one second to come inside and talk to me, I would have hugged you."

"I will be back," Sharpton yelled from the audience.

"I will hug you," I replied.

Al Sharpton and I actually hugged each other as we left the

church, but it was the last I saw of him. I don't think he showed up at another funeral after that.

My experience with Jesse Jackson was very different. I had breakfast with him almost every other day in the weeks following the murders. Initially, I was trying to keep him close so he wouldn't add anything to the media circus surrounding the murders. I know that open communication in times like this is hugely important. It's when people feel left out of the loop that they get frustrated and get loud. I wanted to keep him in the loop about what I and the state were doing to find justice for the victims.

Jesse Jackson and I didn't always agree but we heard each other. He talked about his experiences as an African American, and I told him about growing up Indian American in rural South Carolina. Our backgrounds were different. But we didn't get into a contest over who had suffered the most. We just respected the fact that each of us was doing the best we could to keep others from feeling pain.

I consider Jesse Jackson a friend to this day because he took time to know me as a person. He didn't come into South Carolina and take shots at me just because I was a Republican. He didn't come into my state to stir up trouble. He came in to understand. And once he understood my intentions, he saw that I was just trying to do the best I could in a difficult situation. I came to understand the same about him. Most of all, I came to respect that in a situation in which he could have scored cheap political points, he chose to listen rather than scream. There's a lesson in that for all of us.

NINE DAYS AFTER THE MURDERS, a public memorial service was held for Senator Pinckney at the College of Charleston TD Arena. It was another emotionally moving event. President Obama gave a magnificent eulogy. He spoke eloquently about the history of the black church. He preached about the redemptive power of grace.

"For too long we were blind to the pain that the Confederate flag stirred in too many of our citizens," the president said. "By taking down that flag we express God's grace."

By that time, I had lost count of all the funerals and memorial services I had attended. Each one was an added blow. I wanted to put my arms around all the families and lift them up, but I didn't know how to. Their pain was inescapable. It surrounded me. It got inside me.

I wasn't alone. One day not long after the shootings, Charleston mayor Joe Riley came to visit me. He and I had attended each and every funeral. We had a bond. The ceremonies had affected both of us in ways we couldn't anticipate. I will never forget what he said to me: "Do you hear the music?" he asked. "When I go to bed all I can do is hear the songs and the music." He was talking about the music at the funerals. I felt the same way. It was almost haunting.

The day after the murders, Connecticut governor Dan Malloy had called me to try to warn that this would happen. Dan had been governor when twenty children and six adults were shot and killed at Sandy Hook Elementary School in 2012. I didn't really know Dan, so I was especially touched by his call. He offered his condolences. And then he gave me the kind of advice that only he could give.

"You are getting ready to go through a very difficult time," he said. He warned that if I let it, the grief and the stress would overwhelm me.

"Make sure you take care of yourself. It's important," he said.

"This will take a physical and emotional toll on you. Make sure you have someone you can talk to."

I appreciated his call, but I didn't understand the wisdom of his advice until later. I was governor. My state was in crisis. I had work to do. My gift has always been to focus on what's in front of me, work until I get it right, and never take my eye off the ball. But that gift was failing me after the Mother Emanuel shootings. I could keep it together long enough for a press conference or a meeting, but when I returned to my office I would cry constantly. When I went home at night, I would climb in bed and cry some more. I couldn't eat. I lost over twenty pounds. My press office started getting calls from reporters asking if I was sick or if I had taken up a new exercise routine.

One night my new chief of staff, Swati Patel, and her husband, Dr. Nick Patel, came over for dinner. We got to talking about the funerals and I completely fell apart. Describing the open caskets, the family members falling over the bodies, crying for their loved ones to come back—it was too much. Nick was my doctor, and he told me that I was showing signs of post-traumatic stress disorder, PTSD. It only made me feel worse. I hadn't experienced trauma even close to what the families of the dead had experienced. My suffering didn't compare.

Still, Nick arranged for me to speak to a therapist. I did this once or twice a week for several months. It helped. And Michael was a saint. He listened to me. He knew I hurt and he knew I needed help. I will always be indebted to him for carrying so much of the burden of my pain and helping me heal. In the end, the God who has blessed me and gives me strength when I am healthy was with me when I was broken. By His grace, I made it through. And my faith deepened.

· · ·

MEANWHILE, WE HAD TO GET the proposal to take down the
flag through the legislature. I had been loud about how the police
body-camera bill was proof that my state could come together and
tackle tough issues. But the truth is, I worried whether we could do
that again with the flag. Both sides were so dug in, and so many
outside groups were invested in the issue. The eyes of the nation
were on us. The longer the legislature took to act, the greater the
opportunity for the national media or outside groups to cause a
divide. I warned the legislators that if they didn't act on their own
to convene to address the flag issue, I would use my authority as
governor to force them into session. There were no more excuses. I
made it clear that we had a job to do and no one was leaving until
it got done.

The debate began in the state senate. From the beginning, Senator Pinckney's spirit was felt by everyone. As is tradition, his desk
was draped in heavy black fabric with a single red rose on top. The
outcome of the vote was never in doubt. The senators hadn't just
lost a colleague, they had lost a brother. Their pain was very raw.
They passed the measure overwhelmingly. Senator Paul Thurmond
voted with the majority to remove the flag. It was a powerful sign
of how much the South had changed since his father was governor
in the 1940s.

The debate in the South Carolina House of Representatives was
longer and much more contentious. There was a group of legislators
who were determined to do whatever they could to weaken the bill.
This vote wouldn't go over well in their districts. I got that. The
constituencies that opposed moving the flag were strong, passionate, and loud. I knew the mail I was getting. I could only imag-

ine the pushback these legislators faced from their constituents. I personally knew many South Carolinians who proudly flew the Confederate flag. They do not fit the negative stereotype that non-southerners have of them. This vote put their representatives in a tough spot. I promised the legislators I would help them if the vote became a problem at election time. I told them this was not about the flag but about peace in a state that was on the brink. We had to get South Carolina to a place of healing. This bill was crucial to that.

After much debate and an attempt to swap out the Confederate flag for another with the same historical meaning, members of the house leadership came to me and said they had reached a compromise. I said, what compromise? Either the flag comes down or it doesn't. There's no compromise. But the legislators assured me they had it all worked out. The flag would come down and it wouldn't be replaced with another flag. But the flagpole would stay. This, they assured me, was the only way the bill could pass. The flag would be removed. Everyone could go home and life would go on. It was a win for me, they said.

Now, I served in the South Carolina legislature for six years. I knew how the legislators thought. And I knew what they meant by leaving the flagpole up. They wanted to keep it there, in its prominent position in front of the statehouse, so it would be ready for the day when they tried to put the Confederate flag back up. I was certain of it.

I could have taken the "win" and walked away. The flag was coming down, after all. The national media circus would go away. Life could even go back to normal, for a while. But one day, probably sooner than anyone could anticipate, we would be back to arguing over this divisive issue. Back to dividing South Carolinians.

I told my staff we weren't going to play this political game. There are times for compromise, but this wasn't one of them. I requested a meeting with the house Republican caucus. It was a group I had belonged to in my years in the legislature, but it had never fully accepted me. The members had ways of doing things, like wastefully spending the taxpayers' money without putting their names on the record in support of it. I had called them out on that and ended the practice as governor. They hadn't ever really gotten over it.

I was nervous walking across the statehouse grounds from my office to the caucus room. When I got up to talk in front of the group, I was that ten-year-old kid again, approaching a group of kids on the playground. I knew I had to get past our differences. I had to somehow take politics out of the situation. So I did the only thing I knew to do: I told them the story of my father and the fruit stand, of the owners who called the police, of the humiliation my father suffered. I spoke from the heart.

"I still pass that fruit stand when we are traveling in and out of Columbia. And to this day every time I see it, I feel pain. All of these years later, I still feel pain," I said. "I don't want any child who rides by their statehouse to look at the grounds and feel that pain. I don't want them to see that flag. I don't want them to see a pole where that flag was. I don't want anything to ever go there again."

When I finished, I was angry with myself again. I had become emotional. I had shown weakness to the last people I could afford to show weakness to. But the room was somber and quiet afterward. The legislators agreed to give up on the idea of leaving the flagpole up. But the debate over the flag itself went on. It was heated and it was passionate. I couldn't leave my office. I sat in my conference room and watched every minute of it.

In the early morning hours of July 9, 2015, the house voted 94 to 20 to remove the Confederate flag from the statehouse grounds. At 4:00 p.m. that afternoon, I signed the bill. I used nine pens, one for each of the families of the victims. Hundreds of people crowded into the second-floor lobby of the capitol to witness history in the making. I can't express the relief I felt. I was happy that day had come, but I was sick at what had brought us there.

"This is a story of how the action of nine individuals laid out this long chain of events that forever showed the state of South Carolina what love and forgiveness looks like," I said.

"Twenty-two days ago, I didn't know if I would ever be able to say this again. But today I am very proud to say it is a great day in South Carolina."

They took the flag down the next morning. I didn't want a lot of pomp and circumstance. I thought the ceremony should be respectful and quick. Still, thousands of people showed up on the statehouse grounds to see it happen. No one spoke. Two state troopers lowered the flag. They handed it to an African American trooper, who handed it to the state archivist for placement in the Confederate Relic Room and Military Museum.

And with that, the flag that had flown at the South Carolina capitol for fifty-three years was gone. But I should have known it wasn't going to be that easy. The crane they brought in to remove the flagpole snapped trying to get the pole out of the ground. Such was the determination of the legislators in 2000 for the Confederate flag to remain on the statehouse grounds that they had buried the flagpole deep in several feet of concrete. It took another crane several tries to finally get the pole out.

It was a historic day for South Carolina and the country. It was a day I had prayed for, not just so the flag would come down, but so my state could move forward. After all, the flag didn't kill the

Emanuel Nine. Removing it was important, but that wasn't going
to fix my state. It was the grace and forgiveness of the victims' families that did that.

Two days after the murders, at the killer's bond hearing, the
families of the Emanuel Nine demonstrated the very meaning of
Christian compassion. One by one, they expressed their forgiveness of the man who killed their loved ones. Their grief was fresh
and raw. The killer sat there with no expression. But these amazing
people said they would pray for his soul. It was an act of grace that
stunned the nation. The choice these families made for forgiveness
rather than hate literally made it possible for my state to heal. I will
never be able to adequately express my appreciation and admiration
for them.

The families were humbling in their graciousness, not just on
that day but in the days and weeks to follow. After the flag came
down, I had an American and a South Carolina flag flown over the
statehouse in honor of each of the victims. I gave the flags to each
of the families, but there was one set I needed to deliver in person.

Felicia Sanders had taken her granddaughter to Bible study that
day. When the shooting happened, she lay on top of the girl and
told her to play dead while her son Tywanza was dying next to her.
Felicia also lost her aunt to the murderer. She was one of my heroes.
I didn't know how she managed it, but she was still standing after
the killings—and standing strong.

I went to Felicia's and her husband, Tyrone's, home. They were
kind and welcomed me into their living room. The whole family
was hurting. Felicia managed to be strong but Tyrone was so mad.
Their granddaughter would sneak into Tywanza's room so she could
sleep at night. Felicia couldn't watch television anymore because
gunshots would send her back to that night. And Tyrone couldn't

get the song "Circle of Life" from *The Lion King* out of his head. He had lost his Simba.

I had gone there to honor Tywanza. I had gone to try to comfort his parents. But I burst into tears almost immediately after entering their home. I can't remember what I said. But as I left, I was overcome with regret that I hadn't been stronger for them.

I think Felicia knew how I felt. As I went down her steps to my car, she yelled out to me, "I got to tell him I loved him." Even today, I am so grateful to her for saying that. I had gone there to help Felicia, and she had ended up helping me. Tywanza didn't die alone. He knew his mom was there. And he knew she loved him.

Felicia knew, from one mom to another, how much I needed to know that.

3

The Country Turns to Trump

I couldn't have been more proud of the people of South Carolina. We came through the Mother Emanuel Church murders unified in sadness but uplifted by the grace of the families. And we came through the removal of the flag still respecting each other. We still loved our state. But proud as I was, I couldn't shake off the trauma of everything we'd experienced. It followed me for months after. My staff would say that something about me changed as the result of what had happened. In retrospect, I can see what they were talking about. The tragedy shattered my sense of security about our country. It made me aware of how easily troubled or mentally unstable people can be influenced by others' words.

During his trial, the Charleston killer confessed that it was the Trayvon Martin case, in which an unarmed black teenager was shot by a mixed-race neighborhood-watch volunteer in 2012, that had "awakened" him to his hatred of African Americans. He then went on the internet and became immersed in racist and white nationalist propaganda.

In December, a Charleston jury found the killer of the Mother Emanuel Church victims guilty of thirty-three federal charges, including murder and hate crimes. A month later, it sentenced him with the death penalty.

But the racial anger and identity politics that had inspired the killer only grew in the months after the shooting—not in South Carolina, but in other parts of the country. The wave that had started with Ferguson and Baltimore continued to build. There were more racially charged incidents between white officers and African Americans caught on tape. One woman, Sandra Bland, was pulled over for failing to signal when she changed lanes and ended up dying in police custody. A grand jury in Cleveland failed to indict a white police officer who shot and killed a black twelve-year-old boy who turned out to be holding a pellet gun. At the University of Missouri, the president was forced out by student protests following a series of racial incidents on campus. At Yale University, students erupted over supposed culturally offensive Halloween costumes.

In the midst of all this, a remarkable seventeen different candidates were battling for the 2016 Republican presidential nomination. Five Democrats were running for their party's nomination. The topics of race, law enforcement, and identity became part of the presidential debate. Partisan divides deepened. Republicans became more pro–law enforcement. Democrats went the opposite direction, influenced by the radical elements of the Black Lives Matter movement.

Black Lives Matter activists shut down a meeting of progressive Democrats in July, cutting off Democratic presidential candidate and former Maryland governor Martin O'Malley in mid-sentence. They refused to even allow socialist Vermont senator Bernie Sanders to speak. The candidates' sin, in the eyes of Black Lives Matter, was to say that "all lives matter." This was the depth to which our national debate was sinking. And the movement's hostility to law enforcement was hurting the very people it claimed to represent.

I was disgusted by the whole thing. There are a small number of racist cops who abuse their authority in horrible ways. They must be held to account, as we did in the Walter Scott case. But the vast majority of law enforcement officers are great men and women who do really hard jobs under often dangerous conditions. We owe them our thanks, not condemnation. And we have to recognize who actually gets hurt the most when police are wrongly scapegoated.

During this period I gave a speech at the National Press Club in Washington, D.C., and said, "Most of the people who now live in terror because the local police are too intimidated to do their jobs are black," I said. "Black lives do matter. And they have been disgracefully jeopardized by the movement that has laid waste to Ferguson and Baltimore." I'm so proud that South Carolina reacted to our own horrible racial episodes in a much healthier way.

AT SOME POINT, I WOULD want to endorse a candidate in the South Carolina primary. All the Republican candidates were spending time in the state in advance of the February 2016 voting. I made a point of meeting with or talking with most of them. Michael and I hosted some of the candidates for dinner at the governor's residence.

Florida governor Jeb Bush was one of my guests. In my 2010 campaign for governor, then governor Mark Sanford was an early

supporter of mine. He and I had both fought for openness, accountability, and fiscal conservatism in South Carolina government. But
after Sanford was caught lying about hiking the Appalachian Trail
when he was, in fact, with his mistress in Argentina, his standing in
the state exploded, and my campaign stalled.

It was Jeb who advised me to get out and do something, anything that would get us talking to South Carolinians and engag-
ing with them. It was great advice. When I became governor, I
called him and said, "Okay, so what do I do now?" He sent an
advisor to South Carolina to walk us through getting our offices up
and running. Later, when we wanted to reform K–12 education in
South Carolina, Jeb dropped everything to help me. He was gracious and generous. Jeb was one of the first to visit with us during
the primary season.

Texas senator Ted Cruz and his wife Heidi also came to dinner.
I was impressed with Ted's intellect and his fight. And I was really
impressed with Heidi. She's just as smart as her husband and just as
committed. They are a great team.

Florida senator Marco Rubio also came to see me. Marco and
I had both run as Tea Party Republicans in 2010. We just clicked.
His story was my story. He was also the child of immigrants who
came to America for a better life. And his fight was my fight. He
shared my desire to preserve American values by fighting for them
at home and abroad. There was no way I couldn't totally relate to
Marco.

Of the remaining candidates, I'd known Donald Trump for
several years. When I won the Republican primary for governor
in 2010, he sent me a campaign contribution in a gold-trimmed
envelope. After that, I met him several times in New York when
I was there on business. He seemed to follow my political career.

He would occasionally send me clippings of articles that mentioned me. In 2014, after I was reelected governor, he sent a fax. In very Trumpian fashion, it simply said, "Nikki—You're a winner!" with his signature.

Over the course of the summer of 2015, Donald Trump's campaign for president went from being laughed at by political elites to dominating the Republican debates. He was a serious contender. But something about him held me back. I agreed with his positions on securing our southern border and keeping America safe from terrorism. But his rhetoric in expressing those views turned me off. It took me back to the Mother Emanuel murders. Trump was touching raw nerves. The more he did so, the more I worried that some deranged person might react with violence. I knew that wasn't what he intended, but I was concerned that's how he might be wrongly taken.

WE WERE PREPARING OUR 2016–2017 state budget in December when I got word that Senate majority leader Mitch McConnell and House Speaker Paul Ryan were trying to reach me. I had no idea what they wanted. When we connected on the phone, they told me they wanted me to deliver the Republican response to Barack Obama's last State of the Union address in January.

My first response was surprise. I hadn't expected that request. But my second response was total rejection. There was no way I was going to do that. I called Jon Lerner and told him I had been asked to do the State of the Union response but I didn't think it was a good idea. Do I even need to bring up how former Louisiana governor Bobby Jindal—a friend and respected colleague— had come across in his Republican response? I said. And then there was Marco Rubio—another very skilled communicator—and the "water" incident. Rubio had been mocked for reaching for a bottle of water and taking a big swig in the middle of his remarks. You can't win, I told Jon. There is no way to be effective in a room alone talking to a camera after a sitting president has addressed the nation from a joint session of Congress.

Jon counseled patience—that was really his only play at that point. Step back, he said. Think about it. I said I can think about it all you like, but I'm not going to do it.

I thought about it—and then I ended up agreeing to give the speech. I came to the realization that this was a one-of-a-kind opportunity to talk about the state of our country's politics. It wasn't just one party's rhetoric or Donald Trump's rhetoric. Our politics were getting toxic. The American people didn't trust our institutions, our government, and increasingly, each other. I was certain that we could do better than the Obama administration had done. We could have more jobs, lower taxes, and better schools—if we could resist the temptation to divide into bickering, feuding tribes. I strongly believed we needed to refocus the country on working together to build our strength and not allow ourselves to be torn apart.

I delivered the speech from the governor's mansion in Columbia. I was nervous. It was the first time I had deliberately stepped into the national spotlight. I wore a bright blue suit. But what the camera couldn't see was that I wasn't wearing shoes, just white athletic socks. My staff brought me a "lucky" Gatorade. It was a tradition that dated back to the debate nights during my campaigns. These were little things, but they made me feel better.

After I delivered the speech, my press people were monitoring Twitter and television to see how it went over. The reaction was positive. But there was one review from the media that I really wanted to see, and that was from columnist Charles Krauthammer. Charles died in 2018. He was that one true and wise person. He was a conservative who spoke from a place of love and respect for our country. His review, it turned out, was even better than I could have dreamed.

"It was the best written and best delivered answer to a State of the Union address that I've ever heard," he said on Fox News after the speech. "Even the lighting was good!"

I was happy, not just with Charles's review, but with the message my speech had sent. It was something I believed really needed to be said.

I ONLY HAD TIME TO touch on a few issues in the speech. I decided to devote a portion of it to what was being distorted by both sides: immigration and the controversy over how America was dealing with refugees, particularly people fleeing the bloody Assad regime in Syria.

Immigration is a topic that is personal to me. My parents left behind lives of privilege in India to come to America, and they struggled when they got here. They made that sacrifice so my sister, brothers, and I could grow up in America.

My parents came legally. So it is no surprise that they are offended by those who try to come here illegally. America is a generous and open country; my family experienced that firsthand. But it makes no sense to allow people to break our laws and in return get education, health care, and housing, all at the expense of Americans who are here legally. Misguided policies like establishing sanctuary cities only make the problem worse by undermining respect for the law. A broken system in which children are placed at risk in order to serve as guaranteed admission tickets to the United States also contributes to the crisis. As long as immigrants outside of our country know there are ways to circumvent and take advantage of the system, many will do it.

The left has worked hard to erase the difference between legal and illegal immigration. Their message, which is echoed constantly by the mainstream media, is that if you are for borders you are cruel. If you are against borders, you have a heart. But this is a prime example of the divisive politics that is poisoning our public debate. It's just another version of the "my opponents aren't just wrong, they're evil" style of argument. It's a tactic designed to drive people further apart rather than bring them together to find solutions.

What those pushing this argument don't realize or don't want to acknowledge is that this kind of polarizing, us-versus-them politics actually hurts those immigrants who want to come to America, work hard, respect our laws, and embrace our principles. Equating support for immigration with open borders only causes people to oppose immigration. But the choice isn't binary, and I made this point in my response to President Obama's State of the Union speech.

We are a special country. We believe in protecting human rights. We believe that every child of God has the right to life, liberty, and the pursuit of happiness. But that doesn't mean we have to open our borders to uncontrolled illegal immigration. It's possible to protect our borders and our sovereignty while at the same time remaining true to the principles and beliefs that make our nation exceptional.

How we handle refugees—those immigrants whose lives and

safety are genuinely at risk in their home countries—is at the center of this debate. When I was governor, South Carolina was like other states in taking in refugees. But there was a process we followed to ensure that those refugees were vetted and didn't pose a risk to South Carolinians. We also made sure they weren't gaming our system, that they were truly at risk in their home countries. When we were sure they were genuine refugees, we were generous and welcoming.

When Michael was deployed to Afghanistan, the two Afghan interpreters who worked with his unit literally kept them safe. They fed the unit intelligence and translated the threats and conversations they had with other Afghans. Michael's unit was truly grateful to them, so when its members came home, they worked hard to bring the interpreters with them. If the interpreters had stayed in Afghanistan, they would have been killed for working with the American military. Michael worked with Senator Lindsey Graham and others to successfully bring one of them and his family to South Carolina as refugees. The Lutheran Church was hugely helpful in providing them with temporary housing and English lessons. Today, one of the interpreters works for an organization that helps at-risk youth turn their lives around. He is happy, a citizen, and paying his taxes. He and his family are Americans who lift up other Americans.

This is the way our refugee system is supposed to work. As governor, my first priority was the safety of the people of South Carolina. That's what had been foremost in my mind during every hurricane, the Charleston shooting, and the thousand-year flood of South Carolina that followed. Part of keeping people safe is knowing exactly who we are bringing into our state. Michael and his unit knew their interpreters. They had put themselves at tremendous risk to help American soldiers. They had a genuine fear for their lives. It was absolutely the right decision for South Carolina to welcome them with open arms.

When the brutal civil war in Syria forced more than half of all Syrians to flee their homes, America had to decide how to handle the massive flow of Syrian refugees. But unlike the interpreters from Michael's unit, we knew little about the Syrians seeking to come to America. Nonetheless, President Obama wanted to admit a hundred thousand new refugees, including ten thousand Syrians. Many of these refugees would seek to come to South Carolina. I had to decide for the people of my state whether this was in our best interests. So I went directly to the source at the time: then FBI director James Comey. I asked him point-blank if I should be concerned about Syrian refugees coming to live in South Carolina. His response was telling.

"We don't have any information on the Syrian refugees," Director Comey told me. "We have no background information on them. We don't know if they pose a threat or not."

That was all I needed to hear. We had just learned that one of the terrorists who killed 130 people and injured over 400 more during an attack on a Paris theater had posed as a Syrian refugee to get into Europe. I decided that South Carolina would join in calling on the Obama administration to stop admitting refugees until we knew they were vetted. It was my absolute responsibility as governor. But the federal government and the courts overrode us.

By the time I delivered my State of the Union response, the debate over Syrian refugees had become toxic. There were voices on both sides accusing the other of bad faith. For me, it was always about the best interests of the American people. Our immigration conversation, then and now, should never be about race, religion, or political advantage. It should be about creating a process that allows people to come to this country legally, contribute to our communities, and give back to our country, just as my parents did and just as they always told us to do.

At the same time, the United States can't let our openness and our generosity be used against us. We have to be vigilant about who comes to our country. It only takes one terrorist to slip through the process to cause a massive loss of life. It wasn't that long ago that air travel was much easier. You could see your loved ones off at the airport gate. Security was much less of a hassle: You could keep your shoes on and hold on to your bottle of water. Then 9/11 happened. And America suddenly realized how naive we had been to the threats in the world.

It was the growing polarization in our immigration debate and in our politics in general that inspired the line that the media instantly sensationalized from my speech.

"During anxious times, it can be tempting to follow the siren call of the angriest voices," I said. "We must resist that temptation."

The speculation that this remark was aimed at the media's new fixation, Donald Trump, began immediately. The next morning on the *Today* show, Matt Lauer asked if Trump was who I was referring to. I said his was one of the voices that were making our politics toxic. But so were the media, activist groups on the left and right, even some people in my state of South Carolina.

In response to the same question on *CBS This Morning*, I called out Democrats and Republicans alike. "We've got a responsibility. The way we handle issues and the way we talk about issues should be towards solutions, not division," I said.

What so many in the media missed or chose to ignore was the

message in the speech about how South Carolina provided a model for the nation in detoxifying our politics. In my speech, I mentioned the pain and loss of life from the Mother Emanuel Church murders. But I asked Americans to focus not on the tragedy, but on what happened next.

> *Our state was struck with shock and pain and fear, but our people would not allow hate to win. We didn't have violence, we had vigils. We didn't have riots, we had hugs. We didn't turn against each other's race or religion. We turned toward God, and toward the values that have long made our country the freest and the greatest in the world. We removed a symbol that was being used to divide us. And we found a strength that united us against a domestic terrorist and the hate that filled him.*

Then I turned to the lesson for America.

> *In many parts of society today, whether in popular culture, academia, the media, or politics, there is a tendency to falsely equate noise with results. Some people think that you have to be the loudest voice in the room to make a difference. That's just not true. Often, the best thing we can do is turn down the volume. When the sound is quieter, you can actually hear what someone else is saying. And that can make a world of difference.*

My speech was an appeal, not to pretend we didn't have differences, but to avoid demonizing those we disagree with. Appealing to the worst in our fellow Americans was fueling an endless cycle of cheap political point scoring. It might make some people feel good, but it accomplished nothing constructive. And it was dangerous.

As if to prove my point, sensationalist pundit Ann Coulter tweeted after my speech, "Trump should deport Nikki Haley."

MEANWHILE, THE BATTLE FOR THE Republican nomination for president continued. Seven candidates were on the main stage for the first Republican debate of 2016 in North Charleston on January 14. Donald Trump was there, as were Senators Rubio and Cruz, neurosurgeon Ben Carson, and Governors Jeb Bush, John Kasich, and Chris Christie. I was in the audience watching them spar over the economy, trade, refugees, and other issues when, about a half hour into the debate, my words from the State of the Union speech came back to me again. Fox Business Network's Maria Bartiromo, one of the moderators, mentioned the "angriest voices" comment. Then, referring to me, she asked Donald Trump, "Was she out of line?"

Trump had said some negative things about me the morning after the speech. But we had talked earlier on the day of the debate. I thought we had buried the hatchet, but I wasn't entirely sure. Fox cut to a split screen, with me on one side live from the audience, and Trump on the other side of the screen. I felt the camera on me and tried to smile. Then Trump surprised me—for the first time, but certainly not the last.

"Wherever you are sitting Nikki, I am a friend," he said. "We're friends."

It was an early lesson for me in exactly who Donald J. Trump is. When he gets kicked—or thinks he's gotten kicked—he hollers. But he doesn't take it personally. He can put out a bad tweet about someone on Wednesday and go golfing with that person on Saturday.

I didn't know it then, but this exchange established a pattern for Trump and me that would play out again during the primary. Trump went on to finish second in the Iowa caucuses and then first in the New Hampshire primary and Nevada caucuses. He was on a roll coming into the South Carolina primary when I announced my endorsement of Marco Rubio. It was a tough decision. But in the end, the connection I felt with Marco and our shared belief in the promise of America had made the difference.

"I wanted somebody that was going to go and show my parents that the best decision they ever made was coming to America," I told a crowd in front of a warehouse in Chapin, South Carolina, when I announced my decision.

Ironically, my mom was a Trump supporter from the beginning. After I endorsed Rubio, she told me I had made a mistake. We went back and forth about it. I told her she was my mom, she was supposed to be supportive of me! She replied in her usual unsparing way that she loved me but Trump was saying what needed to be said. As a legal immigrant, she especially appreciated his views on immigration. She had strong feelings about people coming into the country the wrong way. Trump understood that, she said.

My mom must have been on to something. Trump went on to win the South Carolina primary. Marco came in second. After coming in a distant fourth, Jeb Bush ended his campaign.

The next set of primaries was Super Tuesday, on March 1. Eleven states would have Republican primaries or caucuses that day. Marco and I went on the road campaigning. We were joined on the road by South Carolina senator Tim Scott and Representative Trey Gowdy. When we appeared together onstage, the media started calling us a Benetton commercial. We worked hard, and by February 29, the eve of Super Tuesday, Marco had lost his voice. So I took to the stage at a rally in Atlanta to speak for him. For weeks, a point of contention in the race had been Donald Trump's tax returns. He refused to release them, saying he couldn't because they were being audited by the IRS. It was make-or-break time for Marco. The voting was just hours away. So I went for it.

"I'm an accountant. I'm telling you there's no audit that precludes you from showing your tax return," I told the cheering crowd. "Donald Trump, show us your tax return!"

Early the next morning, on Super Tuesday, I got into my car after an event and received a tweet forwarded from my press office.

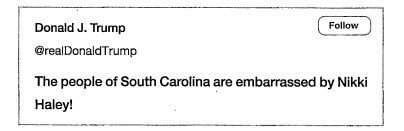

Donald J. Trump
@realDonaldTrump

Follow

The people of South Carolina are embarrassed by Nikki Haley!

Trump had been kicked, and he was hollering. But what he didn't know then was, when I get kicked, I holler, too. When I saw the tweet, the right response just came to me. I tweeted:

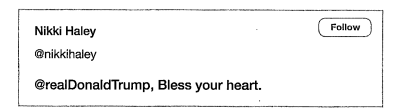

Nikki Haley
@nikkihaley

Follow

@realDonaldTrump, Bless your heart.

It was southern-woman code. Three polite words that let the receiver know you mean something not so polite. One Charleston newspaper called it "the tweet heard 'round the South." Whatever it was, it changed my relationship with Donald Trump. After that, there was a kind of strange respect between us. He knew I was tough and I was going to say what I think. I understood he was the same.

TRUMP WOULD GO ON TO win seven states on Super Tuesday. Cruz won three and Rubio won one. Rubio stayed in the race, and I continued to campaign for him. He was holding out hope for a victory in his home state primary on March 15. But Trump won the Florida GOP primary easily. Minutes after the polls closed, Marco suspended his campaign and dropped out of the race. It had been a hard-fought battle, focused on protecting and preserving the American Dream that had transformed the lives of Marco, me, and so many other Americans.

The next day at a press conference, I was asked who I supported in the remaining Republican field for president. I said I liked and admired Ted Cruz's solid conservatism and that I would personally like to see him win. But I stopped short of endorsing him. Cruz went on to suffer a series of defeats to Trump in the Northeast. Then, after losing Indiana and seeing no way to secure the nomination, Senator Cruz dropped out of the race in early May. The first-term Texas senator who had hoped to run as an outsider against the Republican establishment had lost the nomination to the ultimate outsider, Donald Trump.

It had always been my intention to support the Republican nominee for president in 2016. I supported Donald Trump in the general election. I wasn't loud about it, but I knew how urgent it was for the party to come together to defeat Hillary Clinton.

Clinton's nomination was obviously historic, in that she was the first woman nominated for president by one of the major parties. I didn't know her, although I had met her several years before at a women's professional event in Greenville, South Carolina. At that event, she had inspired me to run for office and make my voice heard. And in some ways she remained inspiring. But I couldn't get past so many of her problems and policies that I thought were bad for the country. As I had made clear during the primaries, I had reservations about Donald Trump, but I had more about Hillary Clinton. I didn't feel bad at all voting against someone who would have been the first female president. I'm absolutely convinced that America will have a woman president someday, and I look forward to that day. Clinton was just not the right woman as far as I was concerned.

I attended the Republican National Convention in Cleveland that summer. I had spoken at the 2012 Republican National Convention on behalf of the Republican nominee, Mitt Romney. My message then was about my family, my state, and how South Carolina was thriving despite the best efforts of the Obama administration. Republican National Committee (RNC) chairman Reince Priebus asked me to speak again in 2016. In the end, we couldn't make it work. I was thrilled, however, to see my fellow governor Mike Pence selected as Donald Trump's running mate. I met Mike when he was elected Indiana's governor in 2012 and I had worked with him in the Republican Governor's Association (RGA) ever since. I considered him a friend. Donald Trump and I had had our differences, but his choice of Mike was something I supported and was comforted by. Most of all, I felt strongly that the party had spoken. We had a Republican ticket. Now it was time to work hard to take back the White House.

As the race between Donald Trump and Hillary Clinton played

out that fall, I listened as the mainstream media and even some of my advisors told me there was no way Donald Trump could win. I didn't claim to know either way, but I had a feeling he might surprise us all.

Then, about ten days before the election, I went to a fundraiser for Congresswoman Barbara Comstock, a friend who represented a district in northern Virginia, just outside Washington, D.C. Barack Obama had won the district narrowly in 2008. Mitt Romney had won it in 2012. It was a true swing district. But at Barbara's event, I was amazed by the passion the people had for Donald Trump. I lost count of how many Republican voters came up to me to say it was critical for the country that Trump win the presidency. I called Jon Lerner. "I know you say he's probably not going to win, but I'm in Virginia and I've never seen anything like this," I said. "Everybody is obsessed with him."

Ten days later, we stayed up all night watching Donald Trump win the 2016 presidential election. As he picked off midwestern and Rust Belt states like Michigan, Wisconsin, and Pennsylvania, it was clear something momentous was happening. I was scheduled to appear the next morning on the *Today* show to talk about the future of the Republican Party. Everyone had assumed it would be an autopsy, an analysis of a Republican defeat. Now it looked like the Republican who had run against the Republican establishment was about to win. What did it mean? I told my press team to cancel the appearance. The truth was, I didn't know what it would mean, and I wasn't going to go on national TV and pretend I did.

Looking back, I can now see that most of the press and the prognosticators thought Trump was going to lose the 2016 election because the things that fueled his victory aren't easily captured in polls or political talking points. It wasn't even about Democrat or

Republican or left or right. Donald Trump won because he reached a culture in America that has felt ignored and voiceless.

He called them the "forgotten Americans." Most of the media and the political elite thought Trump couldn't win because they don't know any forgotten Americans. But I do. I grew up with them in Bamberg, South Carolina. They're proud. They work hard. They're patriotic. They serve in the military. But they've lost faith in many of the institutions of American life. They don't trust the media, the government, Hollywood, the political parties—and most politicians.

In other words, these people are what we in Bamberg would call *real people*. Donald Trump spoke to them. He was blunt, he was confident, and he was direct. Sometimes he was rude and offensive. But he didn't talk in political-speak or focus-group talking points. He said the things that needed to be said. He connected.

Donald Trump also did what his opponent, Hillary Clinton, didn't do. He showed up. He didn't focus on TV ads. He went to the places other candidates ignored.

In the last hundred days of the election, Trump visited Florida, Pennsylvania, Ohio, North Carolina, Michigan, and Wisconsin 133 times. Hillary Clinton visited them far less often. She famously never went to Wisconsin as the Democratic nominee. In the last two days of the election, Trump did ten rallies in six different states. Even if it was eleven o'clock at night, Trump showed up and showed these Americans they mattered.

One night years before, during a tough campaign—my first race for the South Carolina legislature—Michael and I had dinner at a Chinese restaurant. It was a low point, a time when I felt like my fight against the political establishment in South Carolina was impossible to win. As crazy as it sounds, I found a message in a fortune cookie that night that guided me for the rest of that race and all the races since:

Winners do what losers don't want to.

I taped that fortune cookie message to my computer so I wouldn't forget it. I started to go to places that were not necessarily comfortable for me, places where I knew people didn't already support me. I discovered that when you go places that are uncomfortable for you, you grow stronger. This has been the story of my life, over and over. I've always been underestimated. I get into a situation, and everyone says I'm not prepared enough and I can't do it. And I've always responded by diving in, working harder than everyone else, and proving them wrong. I don't let what other people think bother me. I just work.

Donald Trump did what Hillary Clinton wouldn't do, and he proved the truth of that fortune cookie once again. What I didn't know on election night was that I would soon have to do the same.

4

A New Day at the UN

It was November 16, eight days after the 2016 presidential election was upended. I was in Orlando, Florida, at a conference of Republican governors when RNC chairman Reince Priebus called. I texted him back that I was in a working meeting and couldn't talk. I had just been elected vice-chair of the RGA. My friend Wisconsin governor Scott Walker had been elected chairman.

I was excited about what this meant. I would be vice-chair for 2017, and then chairman of the organization for the critical 2018 midterm elections. This was a commitment the RGA had been asking me to make for years, but I never thought the time was right. I've always thought that if you take something on, you have to invest in it and be great at it. If you can't do that, don't do it. Now, with two years left in my term-limited run as South Carolina governor, it was the time to make the commitment. This was my chance to help get good governors elected, to exercise my political muscles and give something back.

I texted Reince:

I'll call you when I'm out of this meeting.

He texted back:

I need you to leave the meeting and call me right away.

Three days earlier, Reince had been named President-Elect Donald Trump's chief of staff. I left the meeting and called Reince.

"The president-elect would like to see you," he said. "He wants you to fly to New York and meet with him tomorrow."

I explained that I was at the RGA. Things were happening. "Why does he want to meet with me?" I asked.

"He wants to talk with you about a position in the administration."

"What position?" I asked.

"Secretary of state," he replied.

I was genuinely taken aback. I didn't know what to say, so I said the first thing that came to me. I told Reince I couldn't be secretary of state. I had just been elected vice-chair of the RGA.

Reince always had a funny way of calling it like he saw it.

"Nikki, really?" he said, exasperated. "Secretary of state or vice-chair of the RGA? This is a tough call for you?"

I saw what he meant. For no other reason than out of respect for the president-elect, I had to go to New York. The next morning, Michael and I flew up to meet him in Trump Tower.

. . .

PEOPLE HAVE ALWAYS LABELED ME with a word that is somehow only negative when it is applied to women: ambitious. But I've never thought of myself as ambitious, at least not in the calculating way many people mean when they use this word to describe women. I don't spend my life thinking about what's next. I focus on my work for the day. Life has taught me that when you work hard and give it your all, doors open. Plotting and scheming about the future seems like a waste of time and energy.

And there is something else that life has taught me: Timing matters. You can be confident and believe in yourself. But you also have to know what it takes to be great at something. You have to know when you're ready and when you're not. I will take chances, sometimes big chances. But I only risk going as far as I know I can be successful. I'm not going to jump into a firepit and say, "Oh it will work out just fine." The job of secretary of state struck me as that kind of jump.

Michael and I arrived at Trump Tower and requested to take the back stairs in order to avoid being seen. Trump Tower was swarming with press by then. We had met with Donald Trump twice over the years when we were in the city for political work. His office was ornate and gold-accented but not as large as I expected.

When I entered, Trump was sitting behind his desk. Reince was there, as were Senator Jeff Sessions and advisor Steve Bannon.

I thanked the president-elect for thinking of me.

He made a sarcastic remark like, "I guess your guy didn't pull it off, did he?"

I laughed. I knew he couldn't resist the dig about Rubio.

Trump asked me about Michael. I told him he was in the lobby, waiting.

"He's here?" he said. "You should bring him in." He sent Reince down to bring Michael up.

Meanwhile, I got to the point. "I really appreciate you asking me to be here," I said. "But I'm not your person."

The new administration needed to come out strong on foreign policy after the Obama years. I believed President Obama and his team had degraded the United States' standing in the eyes of both our friends and our enemies, that he had made the world a less safe place for the American people.

"You should find someone who could really hit the ground running, with no learning curve," I said. "I'm happy to do whatever I can to help in any way."

We went on to talk about restoring strength to American foreign policy. The last administration's approach, the president-elect said, seemed to be to sit back rather than to lead. He made it clear he didn't want that to continue. I agreed. I thanked him again for the meeting and left.

A couple days later, Reince called back.

"I want to throw something out," he said. "Don't say anything. Just think about it:

"U.S. ambassador to the United Nations."

"Reince, I don't even know what the United Nations does!" I said. "All I know is everybody hates it."

He cut me off.

"Think about it," he said. "The president is going to call you and ask you to take the appointment next week."

Timing is everything. My mind immediately began listing the

reasons this was not a good time to take the job. Was I ready to move from South Carolina to New York City? I had never lived north of Charlotte, North Carolina, in my entire life. There were the kids to think about. Rena was a freshman at Clemson, but Nalin was a teenager. He was in the middle of his sophomore year of high school in Columbia. How could I take him away from his friends and teammates to start over in New York City? I knew that Michael had been moved when he was about the same age. It had been a terrible transition for him. Did I want to do that to my son? And then there were my parents. As they had developed health problems, they had been living with my family and me for three years. Everything they had ever known since 1969 was in South Carolina. I would be taking them away from the places and the friends that had defined their life in America.

Last but not least was the ultimate timing question: Did I know enough about foreign policy to represent the United States on the world stage? As governor, I negotiated deals with some of the largest corporations in the world and convinced them to make South Carolina their home. We had brought $20 billion in foreign investment to our state. At that point, South Carolina was building planes by Boeing and making more BMWs than any other place in the world. We had recruited Volvo and Mercedes-Benz, five international tire companies, and the first carbon-fiber plant in North America.

That night, Michael and I sat down to talk it through. I shared my doubts. I couldn't imagine picking up and leaving everything we knew.

Michael was literally surfing around the Web, researching the United Nations. "You should really take a look at this," he said. "I think you would like it." He assured me that all the family questions would work themselves out. And he thought I would do well as U.S. ambassador to the UN. His confidence meant a lot.

I also thought about South Carolina. We had come so far during my six years as governor. Record-breaking job creation and economic development, landmark education and ethics reforms, and of course the flag removal. I didn't want to leave the state in the lurch, but the truth was, I didn't know how much more we could do with two more years. I'm a big supporter of term limits, and the main reason is that I think public officials too often lack the self-awareness to know the right time to leave a post. I had the feeling that I'd accomplished what I could for the state, and I felt really good about that.

But it wasn't just that, either. The Charleston shooting had been followed by a series of other tragedies in South Carolina. Four months after the shooting, it started to rain in South Carolina, and it didn't stop until over a foot had fallen in Columbia and two feet in Charleston. The "thousand-year flood" was what we called it. Dams failed across the state. Seventeen people died. Hundreds were left homeless.

Less than a year later, a fourteen-year-old gunman opened fire at an elementary school in Townville, about forty miles southwest of Greenville, South Carolina. He wounded a teacher, a student, and killed six-year-old Jacob Hall.

Then, just days later, came Hurricane Matthew. Once again, South Carolina was under water. We had to evacuate a million people from the coast. Thousands were left without water and electricity. At least four people died.

Hundreds of South Carolina police officers, first responders, members of the National Guard, and everyday heroes saw my state through these tragedies. And we came through stronger, as better neighbors, friends, and family members. But we also lost precious lives. As I went from tragedy to tragedy, my heart got heavier and heavier. I managed to keep my head in the game and do my job. But the truth is, the ambassadorship at the United Nations was a chance for me to heal my broken heart. It was an opportunity for love, not tragedy, to define my view of my state once again.

Just as Reince had promised, President-Elect Trump called on Monday.

I had come to the decision to be open-minded about the job, but the conditions would have to be right for it to make sense.

I told the president-elect that I would need some adjustments to the offer. He asked what they were.

"Well, I've been a governor and I don't want to work for anyone else. I would have to work directly with you. So I would want this to be a cabinet position," I said.

He said, "Sounds reasonable. Done. What else?"

"I'm a policy girl, and I would want to be in the room when decisions are made," I said. "So I would want a seat on the National Security Council."

He quickly replied, "Done. What else?"

That's when I felt a pit in my stomach. I didn't expect him to respond so comfortably and willingly to what were tough asks.

"Well, sir," I said. "I'm not going to be a wallflower or a talking head. I have to be able to say what I think."

"That's why I want you to do this!" the president-elect answered.

I had no more excuses. The president-elect was completely gracious, respectful, and determined to get his cabinet in place. After I accepted his nomination to be the U.S. ambassador to the United Nations, the first thought I had was that I needed to tell my staff in the governor's office before the news was leaked to the press. This was going to be tricky because they all knew I hadn't been looking for a job in the administration. The news was going to blindside them, and I didn't know how they would react.

I asked the transition team to hold off on announcing the nomination until I had time to tell my staff. The last thing I wanted was for the people who had worked for and sacrificed for and been loyal to me to hear about the nomination from the press or a leak on social media. I gathered them in my office and told them the news. I was going to take the job in New York. But I made them this promise: I would take care of all of them and make sure they had a home.

Some took it hard. There were tears, not simply because I was leaving, but because a family was being broken up. We were a very close team and we had been through so much together. It had been an unusual run of incredible disasters and incredible victories. It was the end of an era. They all loved each other and knew I loved them. This would be the final chapter of "Team Haley" in South Carolina.

My nomination was announced the day before Thanksgiving. The initial reaction from the press was positive. I was one of the earliest cabinet nominees to be named. Neither the secretary of state nor secretary of defense positions had been announced. And, of course, the press consistently noted what was probably the least interesting part of my nomination—that I was female and a minority. Partly due to these very superficial reasons, the initial reviews were so positive that President-Elect Trump called me the next day and said I was making him look good.

Of course, good news in politics doesn't last long. Soon the critics came out saying I had no foreign-policy experience to do the job. Once again I was automatically underestimated. But over the years my reaction to people doubting me has changed. I like being

underestimated, because it motivates me to prove to the people
what I can do for them, and it surprises everyone when they realize
how serious I am about everything I take on. It went back to what
my parents always said to us growing up: "Whatever you do, be
great at it, and make sure people remember you for it."

Still, my critics did have one point. I had a lot to learn before
I could represent the United States at the United Nations. I knew I
had to get myself up to speed on all international issues. So I didn't
waste any time jumping headfirst into a top-down review of the
world and America's interests in it. It felt a lot like cramming for a
foreign-policy exam.

MY FIRST SIGNIFICANT LESSON IN what I would encounter at the UN—the one that affected my ambassadorship more
than any other—didn't come from a briefing book. Exactly one
month to the day after my nomination was announced, the out-
going Obama administration betrayed a friend, and for the worst
possible reasons.

The United Nations has a long, ugly history of anti-Israel bias.
Most of this has occurred in the General Assembly, whose membership includes 193 nations. This is the same body that passed
the infamous 1975 resolution that declared Zionism to be racism—
and broke out into applause when the resolution was passed. The
then ambassador, Daniel Patrick Moynihan, gave an impassioned
speech in opposition to the resolution, but the United States could
do nothing to stop its passage. We were outvoted. There have been
many, many examples of anti-Israel bias in the General Assembly
over the years.

The Security Council is different from the General Assembly, not because it lacks anti-Israel bias, but because its structure doesn't usually allow these resolutions to pass. The Security Council is made up of just fifteen nations. Ten countries are members by election for two-year terms. The five permanent members—the United States, the United Kingdom, France, China, and Russia—each have veto power. Any of these nations alone can prevent a resolution from being passed. It is the United States that has traditionally stopped Security Council actions that unfairly target Israel and hurt the prospect of peace in the Middle East. One of only two vetoes I cast as U.S. ambassador was on a resolution that blamed Israel and Israel alone for Palestinian deaths that resulted from Israel's self-defense against rocket fire into Israel from Gaza. The resolution failed to even mention Hamas, the terrorist group that controls Gaza and orchestrated the attacks. This is typical stuff at the UN.

Prior to my arrival, on December 23, 2016, a shocking event took place. The Security Council approved a resolution, UN Security Council Resolution 2334, that was supposedly meant to condemn Israeli settlements in the West Bank. In fact, the resolution, which was carefully timed after the election so as not to damage Hillary Clinton's presidential bid, did much more. It declared illegal all Israeli activity in *all* the territories that are disputed by the Palestinians. This includes the Jewish Quarter of the Old City of Jerusalem, home to some of the holiest places in Judaism. Resolution 2334 was strategically bankrupt as well as morally repugnant. It damaged the prospects for peace by telling the Palestinians they didn't need to negotiate with Israel. They could count on the Security Council to champion their most ambitious, far-reaching, unrealistic, and unjust goals. What motivation would the Palestinians ever have to negotiate in good faith with Israel when the United Nations was doing their bidding for them?

This was not the first time this kind of resolution had been introduced in the Security Council. But it was the first time in decades that one had succeeded, thanks to the active engagement of the Obama administration. Officially, when the Security Council voted on Resolution 2334, the Obama administration abstained, voting neither yes nor no. In fact, by failing to veto the resolution, they allowed it to pass. And by privately promising Security Council members that they wouldn't veto the measure, the United States affirmatively participated in the resolution's passage.

As a legislator in South Carolina and then governor, I always believed that one of the most cowardly things a lawmaker can do is to abstain. The United States had abstained at the UN on anti-Israel resolutions before but always in response to specific Israeli actions we disagreed with. This resolution was different. It went out of its way to smear Israel and preempt the peace process. For the United States to fail to stand up and take a position on this provocation was a disgrace. The world looks to us for moral guidance; even the countries that say they don't like us count on us for moral leadership. Not only did the Obama administration fail to provide that leadership, it was an active participant in undermining the prospects for peace. It was a sad, sad day for the United States at the UN.

Before I came to the United Nations, I didn't have any particular connection to Israel or the Israeli people. I had never been to Israel or met with any of its leaders. The passage of Resolution 2334 changed that. We had betrayed one of our best friends and closest allies, the only democracy in the Middle East. And we had done so at the United Nations, the place where Israel is continuously scapegoated. But for me, the damage done by Resolution 2334 went way beyond Israel. What kind of message did we send to other countries with this betrayal? We were telling our friends that we couldn't be counted on, that we didn't mean what we say. And we were telling our enemies the same thing. We were telegraphing that the United States wouldn't stand with its friends when things get tough. Going forward, no nation would be deterred by threat of consequences from the United States if it attacked our friends. We had proved we couldn't be relied on to make good on those consequences.

When I got word that the resolution was about to be voted on and that the United States might abstain, I reached out to UN Ambassador Samantha Power. Despite the fact that we had never met, Samantha had been extraordinarily kind and generous to me as I prepared to step into her shoes. She took the time to write up notes on every country in the Security Council. She told me what to expect. And she had made herself available by phone or email any time I needed to reach her.

Now, Ambassador Power wouldn't return my calls or emails. Her sudden silence was mystifying and worrying. It made me think she didn't support what was about to happen. If she had a good explanation for the U.S abstention on Resolution 2334, I thought, she would call me and tell me.

President-Elect Trump immediately denounced the resolution, but there was very little that could be done about it as long as Barack Obama was still president. For me, it was a painful, early lesson in how *not* to represent American interests and values at the United Nations. The Obama administration had gone along with the anti-Israel mob. It would have been harder—and no doubt more lonely—if the administration had stood up to the mob. But it hadn't, and to me it was a cowardly and useless gesture. The United

States had been on the side of the majority, but no good would come from it. The Palestinians and Israelis now had even less reason to negotiate with each other.

MEANWHILE, MY CRASH COURSE IN global affairs continued. I was still governor of South Carolina, so I had to find time at night and on weekends to read, read, and read some more. But what I loved about it was, even with this new challenge, it would be a family undertaking.

I had three whiteboards brought into the governor's residence for me to start keeping notes. I'm a very visual person when it comes to learning things. To my surprise, the morning after they were delivered, I walked into the residence office and there was cute little handwriting on one of the boards. My fifteen-year-old son, Nalin, who was a foreign-policy buff before we went to the United Nations, had made a chart that was split between "countries that are our friends" and "countries that aren't our friends." He had long lists with names of countries on each side. It was a sign that this transition would be a big one for the whole family.

My confirmation hearing before the U.S. Senate Committee on Foreign Relations was scheduled for January 18, 2017. I had to admit this made me nervous. It was the ultimate test of whether I was really learning or just wasting my time. We started making weekly visits to Washington to receive briefings. And we scheduled a series of "murder boards"—mock hearings in which I would be asked the kind of questions I could expect from the committee.

I was overwhelmed, but I leaned back on the habit that had served me well my entire life: I studied. I pushed through the material until I knew it cold. In the first murder board hearing, a series of think-tank experts and academics threw questions at me. It went well. The transition team assigned a grade to how all the presidential nominees were doing in their mock hearings, and mine was high. But just as I was getting cocky about my newfound expertise, we had a second murder board. This time, South Carolina senator Lindsey Graham led the questioning.

Lindsey is an old friend. We had served the state of South Carolina together for years. But on this particular occasion, he showed his friendship by going in for the kill. He was a pro at this stuff. He knew how the senators would conduct their questioning. He didn't just ask one question and then move on. He peppered me with follow-up questions. His pace was rapid-fire. I would be halfway through an answer when Lindsey would interrupt me with another question. It was brutal. But it was for my own good. Afterward, he apologized. "I know that was hard, but that's what you have to prepare for," he said. Then he went to dinner, leaving me and my team behind, having been taken down a few pegs.

I studied even harder than before. We had long days of briefings in a small room in the General Services Administration Building in Washington. We spent a half hour on each subject with only one short break for lunch. I scheduled another, extra, murder board. I did much better. When the actual hearing was held on January 18, I was probably overprepared. But all the preparation had been worth it, because I had my first opportunity to tell the committee how I would approach the job of U.S. ambassador to the UN.

I acknowledged that I was new to international diplomacy—there was no hiding that. But that fact gave me the opportunity to look at the United Nations with an outsider's eyes. And there was another thing I said I would bring to the job of representing the United States at the United Nations:

I will bring a firm message to the UN that U.S. leadership is essential in the world. It is essential for the advancement of humanitarian goals, and for the advancement of America's national interests. When America fails to lead, the world becomes a more dangerous place. And when the world becomes more dangerous, the American people become more vulnerable. At the UN, as elsewhere, the United States is the indispensable voice of freedom. It is time that we once again find that voice.

I was careful not to make too many promises to the committee. But I did make one. The passage of Resolution 2334 convinced me that effective support of American interests and values at the UN required steadfast support for those countries, like Israel, that share our values. Silence was not an option. Even if it meant standing alone, I would always take a stand for America. I told the committee:

I pledge to you this: I will never abstain when the United Nations takes any action that comes in direct conflict with the interests and values of the United States. . . . In the matter of human rights, Mr. Chairman, whether it's the love of my family's and America's immigrant heritage, or the removal of a painful symbol of an oppressive past in South Carolina, I have a clear understanding that it is not acceptable to stay silent when our values are challenged. I will be a strong voice for American principles and American interests, even if that is not what other UN representatives want to hear. The time has come for American strength once again.

I was speaking from my heart and from my gut. I didn't pull any punches with the committee. This was who I was and what I believed in.

Six nervous days passed. Then on January 24, 2017, the Foreign Relations Committee approved my nomination by a voice vote. Hours later, the Senate followed suit with a 96–4 vote in my favor. Suddenly, after months of studying and waiting and uncertainty, time sped up. In a quick ceremony at the South Carolina State House less than an hour after the Senate voted, I resigned my office. Lieutenant Governor Henry D. McMaster took the oath as the new governor of South Carolina.

I was off to New York that night.

5

Taking Names

I've joked that being an Indian American in the rural South in the seventies prepared me to be a Republican in New York in the 2010s. In both cases, I wasn't exactly a part of the establishment. I was the odd woman out, at least for a time.

Michael had moved to New York ahead of me in order to find a new school for Nalin. Out of all of us, Nalin might have been the most eager to take on New York City. He had just finished the first semester of his sophomore year of high school in Columbia. Nalin's only conditions for his new school were that it not require a uniform, that it have a basketball team and be diverse. It was clear right away that life in New York was going to be very different, but we eventually found a great school that fit all these criteria.

It was only later that we found out the school had offered two days of grief counseling after President Trump was elected. We *definitely* were not in South Carolina anymore.

After everyone—including the family dog, Bentley—was moved

into the ambassador's residence across the street from my new office at the U.S. Mission to the UN, I got to work. As the U.S. ambassador, I inherited a group of talented and dedicated foreign service officers. Many would go on to help me negotiate complex deals on behalf of the American people. I relied on their expertise. But I also needed my own team in order to do the job the way I wanted to do it.

I've never had a big circle of advisors. I've always preferred a small, loyal team of trusted people. But I knew the pipeline of administration hires was filling up quickly in those early days of the Trump presidency. Most of the jobs at the UN require high-level security clearances. My staff needed additional clearances to work on the National Security Council (NSC). These security clearance processes are complex and serious. They can take months. I knew I had to act fast in order to get the team I wanted in place.

The problem was, the administration transition office kept pushing me to hire people who had worked on the campaign. It's not unusual for administrations to give campaign workers jobs in government. And I had no reason to think these weren't perfectly competent people. But they weren't *my people*. I didn't want a group of strangers around me. I wanted to hit the ground running with a team of people I knew and trusted. I finally told the director of the Trump transition team that enough was enough.

"I'm not taking y'all's people as rewards for the campaign," I told him. "I have a job to do, and I need my people to do it."

I hated to have to be so direct so early in my new job, but this was a deal breaker for me. When the transition team continued to slow-walk my people through the hiring process, I made a decision to do something that would serve me well throughout my time in the Trump administration: I called the president.

President Trump and I had a newfound understanding of each other ever since the "Bless your heart" incident during the campaign. I was pretty confident he knew I wouldn't call him on a trivial matter. I was also pretty confident he knew I would fight for the ability to do the best job I could. When I told him there were people from South Carolina I needed to bring up to New York, he instantly understood.

"I want you to have your people. You need a good team," he said. "Anyone who is keeping you from doing that, you tell them to call me."

And that was it. The daily calls of people asking me to hire campaign staffers came to an end.

It was the first of many times I would speak to the president directly in order to cut through the bureaucracy and get something done. I did it when I had an idea for a policy. I did it when I needed him to weigh in with a foreign leader. And I did it when I wanted to express my disagreement with him privately. He always took my calls. When he couldn't, he always called back.

This open and honest communication with the president was a large part of the successes we achieved at the UN. In an administration in which so many people's negative relationship with the president was their undoing, my relationship with President Trump was a positive. Our styles were very different, but we were both fundamentally disrupters of the status quo. And we were both action-oriented. When I came to him with a plan to change business as usual at the UN or elsewhere, he most often agreed.

Disrupting was something that came naturally to me long before working at the UN. If ever there was a political system that needed to be shaken up, it was in South Carolina. When I was elected to the South Carolina Legislature in 2004, for example, it was standard practice for the members to pass legislation with a voice vote. There was no roll call. There was no record of who supported or opposed what. There was no accountability. In a business, no sane owner would just hand over her checkbook to some strangers and trust them to spend it wisely. The last straw was when I watched my colleagues vote themselves a retirement pay increase by voice vote. No one ever had to acknowledge voting for the bill—and no one ever did.

I had made it my mission to change this. When I started calling my fellow legislators to let them know I would be introducing a bill that required a roll-call vote on any legislation with a fiscal impact, I got a cold reception. When the house speaker got word that I was trying to end voice votes on spending bills, he not only kicked me off the committee I most cared about, he removed me from the house leadership as well. He did the same to my only friend and cosponsor in the legislature. We were blackballed.

But I didn't give up. I went to the media. I enlisted my friends in the Tea Party to the cause. And soon after I became governor, I signed a bill requiring that any vote with a fiscal impact, and all final votes on bills, had to have a roll-call vote. It was definitely disruptive of the way things had worked for decades, but it was for the good. What we put in place of the "good ol' boy" network was a system that was more accountable to the people of South Carolina. It had cost me dearly as a South Carolina legislator, but it created a check on the ability of legislators to spend the taxpayers' money. And I had learned a valuable lesson: You have to fight for what you believe in. Even when powerful forces challenge you, you have to continue to fight. You can't back down. Ever.

I had the same instinct to disrupt when I came to the United Nations. President Trump called the UN an "underperformer" with "huge potential" and I agreed with him. Its specialized agencies do great things. They feed the hungry, provide health care, and house refugees. But there is also incredible waste, corruption, and bureaucracy at the UN. People have a tendency to interpret any criticism of the United Nations as opposition to its existence. I couldn't disagree more. If I was going to be working at the UN, I was going to do whatever I could to make it achieve its potential. I didn't go to New York to waste my time, and I certainly didn't go to waste the taxpayers' dollars. President Trump and I shared a desire to show the American people value for their investment in the UN. And that meant things had to change.

WHILE MY RELATIONSHIP WITH PRESIDENT Trump was starting strong, my interactions with the new secretary of state, Rex Tillerson, were moving in the opposite direction.

In our first meeting after he was confirmed by the Senate, I told Rex about my hassles with the transition team on hiring my staff. I mentioned that I had finally been able to submit a group of candidates for the White House to review. Before I could go on, Rex quickly said he would be happy to interview them. But, he added, he also wanted to interview two other candidates of his choosing for each position. At first I thought he hadn't understood me. I had identified the people who I wanted, I said, so what he was proposing was unnecessary. I welcomed working with him, but the people around me had to be my choice. I hadn't fought so hard with the transition team just to have someone else tell me who to hire. I didn't want to have to answer to anyone but the president. I didn't need another cabinet member's approval of people I was going to hire, much less have him choose someone else instead.

I left the meeting feeling uneasy. The most important position I needed to fill was that of my deputy. Because I was also a member of the National Security Council, my deputy would be a member of the NSC's Deputies Committee, the highest level of NSC work below the Principals Committee. He or she would be my eyes and ears in Washington, managing all my work with both the NSC and the president's other cabinet members. I had to know and trust this person completely.

There was only one person who fit that bill, and that was my longtime advisor Jon Lerner. I had known Jon for years and worked closely with him. He was very knowledgeable about foreign policy. More important, he knew how I felt about it and would represent my views honestly.

I couldn't believe Secretary Tillerson wanted to hire my deputy. But he did. First he insisted on seeing the résumés of multiple candidates for the position, even after I'd made it clear that Jon was my choice. Then he insisted on personally interviewing Jon for the position, which he did. I ended up hiring Jon, but a bad precedent had been set. I respected Rex for working his way up the ladder at ExxonMobil to become its chief executive. But we just had fundamentally different ideas about our respective positions. I had been a chief executive, too. I thought like one and I acted like one. That was why I had insisted that I be a member of the cabinet and the NSC when I was hired. But from the beginning, Rex had different ideas about how the lines of authority and decision-making would be drawn. He was dismissive of my opinions, and he didn't make any secret about the fact that he believed his views carried more weight.

In contrast, it became obvious to me in the earliest National Security Council meetings that President Trump and Vice President

Pence thought the opposite. They valued my opinion. I think there were a couple reasons for this. First, President Trump always acknowledged that I had good political instincts; years in politics in South Carolina had given me a sense of where the political traps were and how to avoid them.

But more important, the president and vice president valued in me the same thing I always valued in colleagues and advisors: I was direct. I had a point and I got to it quickly. It's one of the most important leadership lessons I've learned: Don't talk for the sake of talking. When you say something, make it matter. If you agree with something, offer ways to make it happen. If you disagree, say so. But always have a plan to find a solution.

In NSC meetings, President Trump frequently would ask for my view. He would listen to Defense Secretary James Mattis and Secretary Tillerson. And then usually he would ask me for my opinion. I would tell him directly and honestly. This seemed to annoy Rex, particularly when I disagreed with him, which I often did.

MEANWHILE, UP IN NEW YORK, I had been thinking about how to introduce myself to my colleagues and to the American people as the new ambassador. Many of the diplomats I would come to meet and work with had been in foreign service for many years. In the world of international diplomacy, being an ambassador to the UN is a very senior position. My new colleagues were all very seasoned. More important, many were trusted advisors to the leaders of their countries.

Before taking the position, I kept going back to the Obama administration's parting actions at the United Nations. They had not only betrayed Israel with Resolution 2334, they had also abstained

on a resolution blaming the United States for the poverty and oppression in Cuba. The administration basically accepted our fault
for the suffering of the Cuban people, which is unthinkable to me.
Both resolutions where the kind that are popular at the United
Nations because they target Israel and the United States, the UN's
favorite punching bags. It was clear to me that the Obama administration had gone along because they wanted to be liked. They
thought they could curry favor with other countries by joining
in bashing Israel and the United States. I thought this was a pro-
foundly self-defeating strategy. The anti-American and anti-Israel
mobs at the UN get their way because they're bullies. And you can't
stop a bully by giving in to his demands.

It had been this way for far too long at the UN. There are few
topics at the UN more popular than America's sins, either real or
imagined. Given the chance, the only issues the UN would consider,
other than the alleged guilt of the Israelis, would be the 1953 coup
in Iran, the Bay of Pigs Invasion, the Abu Ghraib abuse scandal—
anything that highlights the supposed crimes of the United States.
This approach had worked on the Obama administration. It made
its people feel guilty. I thought it was important to let the world
know those days were over.

The first time I set foot in the United Nations Headquarters at
405 East Forty-second Street, I was there to present my credentials
to the UN secretary-general, António Guterres. It was a diplomatic
formality, the way ambassadors officially convey that they are representatives of their governments. The plan was to go meet the
secretary-general, take some photos, and leave. We had been told
that there was a large media contingent waiting outside the elevator
in the lobby, but we had no plans to address them.

As I was walking into the meeting, members of the press started shouting questions at me. My gut told me to stop. This would be a good opportunity to set the tone for my ambassadorship. And there was no better time than the present. I wanted everyone to know that things were going to change for the United States at the UN. The new administration's approach would be different; it was better that everyone knew that at the outset. We were going to stand up for our values and our allies. We were going to act in good faith. We would be honest. We would be cooperative. But we were going to insist on accountability.

"Our goal with the administration is to show value at the UN, and the way that we'll show value is to show our strength, show our full voice—have the backs of our allies and make sure our allies have our backs as well," I told the reporters.

"For those who don't have our backs, we're taking names," I said.

"There is a new US-UN."

My remarks shocked many of my new colleagues and even surprised my staff. The media called them "disruptive," which was good because I meant them to be. I wanted countries to know the United States wanted to build strong relationships with them. But relationships go both ways. I wanted my new colleagues to know they couldn't stab us in the back and think there would not be consequences. They couldn't hold their hands out for our assistance and think it would be business as usual. I wanted those countries that told us one thing and did another, those so-called leaders who yell "Death to America," and those who vote against us and then expect us to act like nothing has happened—I wanted them to know we would no longer be putting up with it. I had an obligation to the American people to make their investment in the UN worthwhile. If I couldn't do that, I would have to make it clear that our investment should change.

The press made a big deal about those two words, "taking names." I had used them before as governor. It was my way of reminding the legislators that I was paying attention and I would remember who had stood up for the interests of South Carolinians and who hadn't. But it quickly became apparent that the UN was not used to this kind of talk, at least not from the American ambassador. That first press conference shook up the typically sleepy UN press corps. Veteran press aides at the U.S. Mission told us they hadn't seen so much media interest since the Iraq War.

My new colleagues on the UN Security Council didn't quite know what to make of it, either. I asked the British ambassador if he had any pointers for me as the newest representative on the Security Council. He said he did. Everyone was pretty concerned about the way I had been talking about "taking names" of countries that didn't support the United States, he said. His implication was clear: I should tone it down and try to play nice with others.

It was a reminder that maybe I wasn't much of a diplomat. But I also thought that instead of changing my ways, maybe the UN should change its ways. I have always gotten my back up when the United States is disrespected. So I made myself this deal: I would observe all the diplomatic niceties. I would smile and be gracious at receptions. But in the end, I was at the United Nations to do a job. The United States was not going to get pushed around anymore, at least not on my watch.

I spent a lot of those first weeks getting to know my new colleagues. All my introductory meetings took place in each of the country's missions. In these meetings and all my subsequent visits, it was fascinating to see how the missions all reflected their country's unique cultures and personalities. At the Ethiopian mission, I was given a gift of coffee. All the African missions were relaxed and welcoming. They had obvious pride in the beauty of their countries and their people. But they were also direct about the challenges they faced. Every time I visited, the Russian mission was also true to its country's personality. We would sit in a parlor and alcohol would be served. It was relaxing, but at the same time I got the feeling we were being watched. We usually left with a bottle of Russian vodka.

Other countries were more formal in their approach. From the first time I visited to the last, the diplomats at the Chinese mission put me in a waiting room by myself before our meeting. I had been warned beforehand to never take my cell phone into the building for fear it would be compromised. After ten or fifteen minutes of waiting, an aide would come and escort me up to the ambassador's office. Then there were diplomatic niceties and Chinese tea. The Turks were also less than warm in their welcome. At our first meeting the Turkish ambassador gave me an hour-long history lesson on the relationship between the United States and Turkey. He made it clear that when it came to the Kurds, the United States was wrong and Turkey was right.

Before I came to the UN, Samantha Power had insisted to me that the order in which I first met with the ambassadors from other countries mattered a great deal at the UN. It sent important messages to other countries about our priorities. For the United States, as one of the permanent five members of the Security Council, tradition dictated that my first visits be with the other permanent members—the United Kingdom, France, China, and Russia.

We decided to send a message by going another way. I thought it was important to visit our friends first. For me, signaling new strength and clarity in U.S. leadership at the UN was more important than diplomatic protocol.

First, I spent over an hour with the British and the French ambassadors, introducing myself and getting to know them. Then I ditched protocol and met with the ambassador from Israel, Danny Danon. Seeing Danny in person gave me an opportunity that I had wanted for some time: to know what the passage of Resolution 2334 had been like from his perspective.

Danny said he knew something was going on in those last weeks of the Obama administration, he just didn't know what. He and his colleagues tried for days to reach out to Ambassador Power and everyone they knew in Washington. No one would take their calls. No one would return their messages. The United States had literally stopped talking to Israel.

The most painful part of our conversation was Danny's recounting of the vote itself. When a non–Security Council member country, like Israel, is the subject of a Security Council vote, its ambassador sits at the huge C-shaped table with the Security Council members. So when Resolution 2334 was passed, Danny was right there. Disgustingly, all the ambassadors at the table stood up and applauded after the vote was tallied. The audience cheered. And in the middle of it all was the Israeli ambassador, remaining seated while the council applauded his country's humiliation. As Danny told me about it, all I could think was how that feeling was all too familiar to me. I know what it feels like to be different, humiliated, and ostracized for being who you are.

Tradition dictated that our next introductory visits be with the ambassadors from Russia and China, the remaining two permanent members of the Security Council. Instead, I decided to go see the ambassador from Ukraine, Volodymyr Yelchenko. Just as Ambassador Power had said, I was making a deliberate statement. And that statement was that the United States was not going to overlook Russia's violations of other countries' sovereignty and democracy. We stood with the people of Ukraine in the face of Russia's ongoing aggression.

I found Volodymyr to be a genuinely kind man. He was one of the United States' best friends on the Security Council, and we in turn supported Ukraine whenever we could. We talked openly about the friction between Ukraine and Russia at the time. Almost exactly three years earlier, Russia had invaded and occupied Crimea, a part of Ukraine on the Black Sea. Soon after, Russia began to encourage rebel fighting in Eastern Ukraine as well. In response, President Obama leveled sanctions on Russia, including on individuals close to Russian president Vladimir Putin. I assured the ambassador that the United States was Ukraine's friend and would stand by his country in the face of Russian aggression. Russia's actions were flagrant violations of Ukraine's sovereignty, not to mention a violation of the very purpose of the United Nations.

Ambassador Yelchenko was quiet one-on-one, but there was nothing shy about him when he represented his country in the Security Council. Ukraine was a rotating member of the council at the time. Volodymyr called a meeting on February 2 to consider Russia's ongoing aggression in their country. The meeting was being watched closely because it would be the Trump administration's first statement on Russia and the Ukraine crisis. No one really knew what the new administration's Russia policy was. There was a lot of media speculation that Trump would act to ease the sanctions against Russia.

It was my first Security Council meeting as the U.S. ambassador. It started a tug-of-war with the Department of State that would go on for most of my ambassadorship. State expected to write my remarks. I expected to write my own. I had my own way of communicating, one that was rarely reflected in remarks drafted by committees of bureaucrats. This was a subject—Russia's illegal activity in Ukraine—that I strongly believed needed clarity for the American people. I was happy to give the State Department and the National Security Council advance copies of my remarks, but my words had to be my own.

Some people thought my remarks were controversial. Many were surprised by my adamant tone. But for me, it was a no-brainer. What Russia had done and was doing in Ukraine was inexcusable. Anyone who thought the United States was going to give Russia a pass on its aggression was wrong, plain and simple.

Everytime I spoke at the UN, I was speaking directly to the American people. This time, I also spoke to the people of Ukraine.

"The United States stands with the people of Ukraine, who have suffered for nearly three years under Russian occupation and military intervention," I said.

"The United States continues to condemn and call for an immediate end to the Russian occupation of Crimea. Crimea is a part of Ukraine. Our Crimea-related sanctions will remain in place until Russia returns control over the peninsula to Ukraine."

Many people in the press approved of my remarks because they thought they were in defiance of the president. Any time the press thought I, or anyone else in the Trump cabinet, disagreed with the president, it ran wild with that "story." This would not be the last time the media pursued its favored narrative instead of the more complicated reality. The truth was much different.

President Obama had talked a tough game but had refused to

provide Ukraine weapons to fight off Russian-backed separatists. The Trump administration did the opposite. In my view, the president's words were far too forgiving of Russia. But the policies he implemented left no confusion over who was our friend and who was our enemy. Our policy, in the end, was much tougher on Russia and much more supportive of the Ukrainian people. The Trump administration provided Ukraine the anti-tank weapons President Obama denied them. We not only kept the existing sanctions in place, we leveled additional sanctions against Russia. We began training Ukrainian soldiers and providing additional weapons.

Russia was a particular problem for me throughout my time at the United Nations. Russia has the ability, just as the United States does, to veto any resolution in the Security Council. And this fact points to the fundamental shortcoming of the United Nations: Some of its most powerful countries do not share our values. They don't share our commitment to freedom, democracy, and human rights. Russia certainly doesn't.

Russia used its veto power when I was ambassador to protect tyrants from Syria to Iran to Venezuela. Russia, along with China, opposed our push to have the Security Council include the violation of human rights in its mandate to protect peace and security. And, needless to say, Russia prevented the Security Council from doing anything about its own illegal annexation of Crimea.

It didn't help our cause that, when I first came to the UN, the Russian ambassador was a seasoned and skilled diplomat named Vitaly Churkin. Vitaly had been a child actor in the Soviet Union and would react with exaggerated drama to the smallest of slights. Vitaly had another quality that was rare to see in the Security Council. He could speak off the cuff. While most of the ambassadors were what we called "stuck to the paper"—that is, they didn't stray beyond their prepared, written remarks—Vitaly could engage directly with others on the Security Council. As I noted before, Vitaly died tragically after my first month at the UN, but he was a formidable character for me, as the newest member of the Security Council, to encounter.

I used his skills as a motivation to match his expressions of Russian strength with my own expressions of American strength. I had learned as governor that tone matters. Tone lets people know if you're serious or if you're going to waffle. Tone lets people know when not to mess with you. I look back now and realize that my ignorance of the "proper" tone to use at the UN was one of my greatest assets. I thought it was important to let Vitaly and everyone else know that it was a new day for the United States at the UN. Things were going to be different. So I didn't worry about what was proper or diplomatic. I just said so.

The UN works best when it is guided by the principles of the rule of law and by respect for the inherent dignity of every human being. Another way of saying it is, the UN works best when the United States is not afraid to be strong and to lead. That determination to lead had gone missing during the previous administration. The Obama administration diplomats seemed to believe that U.S. leadership did more harm in the world than good. But in the early spring of 2017, I was about to learn that, despite other countries' many statements to the contrary, they welcome our leadership.

6

Red Lines and Dictators

I had been at the United Nations for about two months when, early in the morning of April 4, 2017, when most people were still asleep, Syrian warplanes appeared in the sky above the rebel-controlled Syrian village of Khan Sheikhoun. It was not the first time the Syrian dictator, Bashar al-Assad, had sent his warplanes to bomb his own people. But this time, the barrel bombs dropped on the village produced a yellowish cloud that witnesses described as a "winter fog." First it stung their eyes. Then their noses began to run. Their mouths began to foam. Their pupils constricted. They vomited. And then, for the children, women, and men who were most exposed, their bodies went into convulsions, then paralysis. Then death.

Americans woke later that morning to images on the internet and in the media of the dead in Khan Sheikhoun. Over eighty died. Not only did their assailants torture these people with chemical weapons, they bombed the hospitals where victims were receiving treatment. To say it was barbaric is an understatement.

Twelve children literally suffocated to death in their own body fluids. As a mom, it was these pictures that hurt me the most. The children were foaming at the mouth, suffering convulsions, and being carried in the arms of desperate parents. We saw rows of lifeless bodies, some still in diapers.

The United States was presiding over the Security Council that month. Along with France and Great Britain, we immediately called for an emergency session for the next day. I was angry. The blood of the victims of Khan Sheikhoun wasn't just on Assad's hands, it was on the hands of the Russians as well. Using their veto and intimidating other members, the Russian delegation had for years shielded the Syrian regime from any consequences for its actions. They absurdly claimed that any chemical weapons used in Syria were coming from the rebels fighting the Assad regime, not the regime itself. Their claim was laughable. But they stuck with it. Even behind closed doors, when the cameras were off, the Russians refused to admit that Assad was responsible for chemical attacks on civilians.

By the time we met to consider the killings at Khan Sheikhoun, the Russians were stand-ins for the Assad regime on the Security Council. They liked to claim superpower status, but it was Assad, not Putin, who was dictating Russia's Syria policy.

Before I came to the UN, the Security Council had voted unanimously, with Russian support, to create an impartial panel of experts to identify and hold accountable those who use chemical weapons. But once this panel started to determine that it was the Russians' ally Assad who was, in fact, responsible for using chemical weapons against the Syrian people, the Russians decided they didn't like this system anymore. We spent months negotiating with them, trying to save this panel, and with it the concept of holding the Syrian regime accountable for murdering its people in one of the ugliest ways imaginable.

The Russians fought us every step of the way. They claimed to want only an impartial determination of the truth. In fact, they wanted only to protect Assad. During one of our marathon negotiation sessions, I had to be in Washington for cabinet business and missed the first two days of talks. The negotiations were occurring behind closed doors, in the Consultations Room next to the Security Council.

I came back to New York as soon as I could to rejoin the negotiations. When I walked into the Consultations Room, the Russians were enraged. They told me I hadn't been there, and I couldn't join the conversation now. The Russians had spent two days trying to water down the resolution to the point that it was basically meaningless. They would change words to make the language vague. They would always try to draw out the debate until everyone just wanted to get out of there. It was the Russian way to delay and distract. Many of the other ambassadors knew to be suspicious of the Russians, but they often gave in because of exhaustion and frustration. I didn't get exhausted and frustrated. I was determined not to let them succeed in their games.

For two days, my staff had observed the Russian ambassador leave the room to talk to some men outside. Then he would come back in and continue to obstruct the workings of the panel. My staff investigated further and figured out that the men outside were representatives of the Assad regime. The Russian ambassador wasn't going outside for a smoke. He was literally taking his marching orders from the Syrians. I had my staff take a picture to document these "consultations."

Then I called the Russians out in front of the council.

"Do you know what the Russians are doing right now?" I said. "They're making sure the Syrians are okay with what we're doing.

"We aren't debating the Russians," I said. We're debating the Syrians." And I showed them the pictures to prove it.

I would love to say there was shock in the room. But the emotion I saw on most of the ambassadors' faces was more like resignation. This is what they had come to expect in dealing with Russia and Syria. If anything, they were surprised the Russians had been so careless that they got caught taking orders from the Syrians.

Of all the daily irritants and frustrations about working at the UN, the tendency to put talking over acting—the Russian's favorite tactic—was the hardest for me to stomach. I would get impatient with the lack of concrete progress. I wanted to see results. Too many people at the UN measure value by the number of meetings that are held, not in the solutions that are enacted. Sometimes my impatience would come out in abruptness. Especially early on, I was guilty of occasionally cutting off speakers who were reciting the same old talking points.

Sometimes my impatience came out in attempts at humor (a risky move at the UN!). During another one of our endless negotiating sessions on Syria, the Russian ambassador kept stalling by saying it was just too soon to act. The time wasn't right, he said, over and over. This was a familiar tactic that I had seen enough of.

I was at a table of all men. I don't know why I thought they would possibly get the analogy, but somehow I had to push back on the Russians' insistence that the time wasn't "right."

"It's like being pregnant," I said. "There's never a right time to do it, but you're always happy you did."

They looked at me. Some of them laughed. They were getting used to me being passionate. I think at times I exhausted them. But we did succeed in changing the culture of complacency a little bit. After I left the UN, Michael and I attended a dinner with some of the council members. They told us my name sometimes came up when negotiations started to bog down. People would say, "What would Nikki Haley do?" The council missed us, they said. The energy was missing. It was heartening to hear.

HARD AS IT MAY BE to believe, I have a twenty-four-hour rule. I learned this about myself during my time in the South Carolina legislature. Whenever I can, I check my immediate instinct to respond. In the most stressful situations, it's best to wait twenty-four hours before you return fire, if you can. In the heat of the moment, things run through your head. Emotions run wild, and your instincts are soft. Waiting twenty-four hours allows you to pick and choose your battles.

The day we received the news of the Khan Sheikhoun killings, I was outraged—outraged and fed up. As we prepared for the next day's emergency session, I asked my staff to print copies of some of the pictures of Assad's victims. I didn't know what I would do with the pictures, if anything at all. I just knew that the faces and bodies of those tortured children were impossible to get out of my mind. They were a very powerful reminder that evil exists in the world.

The next morning, the emergency session of the Security Council convened. That month the United States held the rotating presidency of the council, so we spoke last. The statements of the French and British ambassadors were strong and on point. The ambassador of the United Kingdom, Matthew Rycroft, talked about Russia's and China's veto just weeks earlier of a resolution to hold Assad responsible for using chemical weapons. The Security Council could have proved its usefulness by sending the clear signal that there would be consequences for use of these weapons. "But after Russia and China vetoed, it seems the only message sent to Assad was one of encouragement," Matthew said. "And yesterday, we saw the consequences of those vetoes."

The rest of the ambassadors' statements were more typical of the UN. China professed itself "shocked" at the use of chemical weapons. Everyone condemned the use of chemical weapons by "any party"—carefully avoiding mentioning the only party that mattered that day, the criminal Assad regime.

My staff had gotten the photos of the victims I had asked for. After the meeting had already started, they brought them from our office to the Security Council in a bag used to transport classified documents. The pictures were smaller than I would have liked, but the gruesome images of the dead children were unmistakable. When it came time for the Russian ambassador to speak, he had the audacity to claim that the victims in Khan Sheikhoun were the result of a Syrian air strike on a weapons warehouse that had accidentally hit a rebel chemical-weapons production facility. It was amazing how emotionless he was. How could the Russians in good conscience partner with an evil dictator, and then be okay with what he had done? They were talking about the victims like they weren't real, like they were things and not people. They needed to see that each victim was someone's child. They needed to see their faces. I hadn't initially been sure I would use the photos. But when it was my turn to speak, I decided to go for it.

I began my remarks by describing the images in the news we had woken up to on April 4. UN protocol is that ambassadors never stand up when they're speaking to the Security Council. But I wanted to make sure everyone in the room saw the pictures, so I stood and held them up as I talked. The Syrian ambassador shuffled his papers nervously and kept his eyes down. I looked straight at the Russian ambassador as I said, "We cannot close our eyes to these pictures. We cannot close our minds to the responsibility to act."

The credibility of the Security Council was on the line. If it couldn't act to stop something the world had already come together to condemn in the Chemical Weapons Convention, why should it exist at all? Ambassador Rycroft was right. Every time the Russians used their veto to protect the Syrian regime—every time the UN failed to back up its own resolutions condemning his behavior—the world was giving a green light to Assad to brutalize his own people.

Worst of all, for me, was the fact that the United States was also guilty of appeasing Assad.

In August of 2012, President Obama had declared that Assad's use of chemical weapons in the Syrian war would be a "red line" that triggered a U.S. military response. A year later, Assad bombed a Damascus suburb with warheads filled with chemical weapons. Over fourteen hundred people died, nearly five hundred of them children. Assad had clearly crossed President Obama's red line. But instead of taking military action, the Obama administration concluded a deal that called for Syria to destroy or remove all its chemical weapons by mid-2014. Guaranteeing Syrian compliance with the deal was, unbelievably, Russia, Assad's closest ally and enabler.

The agreement was a sham. After all of Syria's chemical weapons had supposedly been done away with, Assad went on to use those banned substances hundreds of times, by some reports.* The Obama administration agreement with Syria was just as good as Assad's word, which is to say it was useless. The Russians' word, it turned out, was no better.

The Khan Sheikhoun strike was different from Assad's previous chemical-weapons attacks, however. The weapons used by Syria since the useless agreement had been less lethal but still-monstrous chemicals like chlorine and mustard gas. The gas that rained down on Khan Sheikhoun was the deadly nerve agent sarin, the same chemical that killed hundreds of Syrians in the Damascus suburbs in 2013. After all the lies and all the failed promises, Assad had returned to his poison of choice.

Another thing was different about the 2019 strike: There was a new administration in Washington. The day of the strike, I spoke to the president. We had all seen the horrible images on television and social media. The pictures clearly affected President Trump. He shared my desire to be clear and definitive in the Security Council the next day. President Obama had sent a dangerous signal to the Syrians and the world when he failed to act. It was critical that we send the opposite message.

In my remarks to the Security Council the day after the attack, I challenged Russia to stop its appeasement and protection of the Assad regime.

"If Russia has the influence in Syria that it claims to have, we need to see them use it," I said. "We need to see them put an end to these horrific acts."

---

*https://www.npr.org/2019/02/17/695545252/more-than-300-chemical-attacks
-launched-during-syrian-civil-war-study-says; https://www.gppi.net/media/GPPi
_Schneider_Luetkefend_2019_Nowhere_to_Hide_Web.pdf

Then I glared at the Russian ambassador. "How many more children have to die before Russia cares?"

I ended my remarks with this warning: "When the United Nations consistently fails in its duty to act collectively, there are times in the life of states that we are compelled to take our own action."

Less than forty-eight hours later, President Trump ordered two U.S. Navy destroyers in the eastern Mediterranean to launch fifty-nine cruise missiles at the Syrian air base from which the Khan Sheikhoun attack originated. The strikes hit Syrian aircraft and a refueling facility, destroying 20 percent of Assad's working air force.* But more important than the damage inflicted on the Syrian war machine was the message the strike sent, not just to Syria and Russia, but to North Korea and Iran as well. The United States was back. We would give diplomacy every chance to work, as we had multiple times with Russia and Assad. But in the end we would defend our interests. And we would enforce our red lines.

What was most fascinating about the aftermath of the U.S. air strike was the number of ambassadors who texted me, called me, or took me to the side in the Security Council to tell me it was good to see the United States leading again. It was the first time I realized that behind all the America-bashing at the UN is a genuine desire, even a need, for the United States to lead. At the end of the day, when the world needs a moral compass to guide them, it's not Russia countries look to. It's not China. It's us.

THE DYNAMIC WAS SLOWLY CHANGING at the UN. Our response to Assad's attack had shown new U.S. strength. My colleagues

---

*https://www.whitehouse.gov/briefings-statements/statement-president-trump-syria/

were beginning to sit up and take notice. We capitalized on that strange new respect by using our presidency that month to enact two changes that were badly needed at the UN: reform of its peace-keeping operations and putting human rights at the center of its agenda.

Reform of UN peacekeeping was something I wanted to tackle because peacekeeping is one of the areas of greatest potential for the UN. And yet, when I got there, peacekeeping programs were bloated and inefficient. They too often failed to protect the civilians they were supposed to protect. There was evidence that peacekeepers were less likely to protect civilians from attacks by rebels than by government forces. And they were plagued with instances of soldiers sexually abusing and exploiting civilians. Women and girls who sought protection at UN peacekeeping missions were instead being raped.

The United States was already paying a disproportionate share of the peacekeeping budget. We were determined that our tax dollars were not going to be wasted on peacekeepers who failed to protect civilians and, even worse, exploited and abused civilians. We succeeded in creating concrete, binding steps to strengthen the accountability of our peacekeeping missions.

When we started taking the lead on reforming peacekeeping missions, others began supporting us. For too long, in addition to their other problems, UN peacekeeping missions had been treated like employment projects for troop-contributing countries and international bureaucracies. Going forward, soldiers would now be trained, have a mission that was doable, and have an exit strategy. We were going to focus peacekeeping missions on going in, doing their job to protect civilians, and then going home.

Respecting human rights was something I fought for my entire time at the UN. Initially, no one else in the administration was taking the initiative to talk about human rights. I thought human rights were important for two reasons. First, it's the right thing to do, and it's the *smart* thing for the United States to emphasize. The world's knowledge that we respect freedom and human dignity is one of our greatest foreign-policy assets. Just as people did when we struck back against Syrian chemical-weapons use, the world looks to us to set the standard for human dignity and the rights of women, children, and religious and ethnic minorities. When we fail that standard, it gives others license to do the same.

The other reason to take human rights seriously is because human rights abuses, if they are left unaddressed, inevitably lead to conflict. Abuses spur conflict that starts within a country's borders but often spills over into the broader region and even the rest of the world. Despite this fact, the United Nations Security Council does not consider human rights to be worthy of its consideration. The thinking is that peace and security are the council's business and human rights should be left to other UN agencies, like the Human Rights Council (HRC), an agency so corrupted by members who violate human rights that it is unworthy of its name.

We started to change that, beginning with the U.S. presidency of the council that April. The United States held the first Security Council meeting ever devoted exclusively to human rights. Over the course of our time at the UN, we brought in North Korean dissidents to tell their stories. We tried to bring in political opponents of the socialist Maduro regime in Venezuela, but the Russians blocked us. I met with Amal Clooney and Nobel Prize winner Nadia Morad in New York to shine light on the grotesque victimization of Yazidi women by ISIS terrorists. I met with the Goldins, the family of an Israeli soldier whose remains are being held captive by

Hamas in Gaza. I developed an ongoing relationship with Cindy and Fred Warmbier, the parents of Otto Warmbier, who was tortured and murdered by the North Korean regime.

Syria was a special focus of our human rights campaign. I brought members of the Security Council to the U.S. Holocaust Memorial Museum in Washington, D.C., to see an exhibit on Assad's systematic human rights atrocities. The exhibit told the stories of Assad's victims. It was called *Syria: Please Don't Forget Us*—a message I thought the Security Council needed to hear. I also gave speeches on human rights violations in South Sudan and Burma at the Holocaust Museum. We took the initiative at the UN to fulfill America's role as the voice of the persecuted and oppressed.

I WANTED TO TOP OFF the U.S. presidency in April with a strong message to my fellow Security Council members about our new approach to the United Nations. I was coming to the realization that the United Nations was an organization through which we could actually move American foreign policy. We could have a real impact. But the Security Council had to know that when I spoke, I spoke for the president.

I asked President Trump if I could bring the members of the council to Washington to meet him, and he agreed. I brought all fourteen ambassadors down for the day, including their wives (they were all men at the time). We had meetings on Capitol Hill, and the ambassadors had one-on-one meetings with President Trump.

After that, we hosted a working lunch with the president in the White House State Dining Room. National Security Advisor H. R. McMaster was seated to the president's left, and Michael and I were seated to his right. President Trump spoke frankly about the UN's challenges but also talked about its unfulfilled potential. He generously thanked me for my work. Then he asked the council members an unexpected question.

"Now, does everybody like Nikki?" the president said as the group chuckled nervously. "Because if you don't, she can easily be replaced."

I laughed. The usual suspects in the media immediately speculated that the comment was a not-so-veiled threat: Don't cross me or you'll get shown the door. But it was just one more example of the media's failure, or refusal, to understand the way the president operated. He liked to poke fun at people. The truth is, if he didn't joke and act lighthearted around you, you were likely on his watch list. He didn't want me to get too comfortable. He never did with anybody. But I took his joke as a comment on the strength of our relationship. I was being true to what I had told him when he hired me: I was no wallflower.

The ambassadors were supposed to go directly from the lunch to meetings with McMaster and Middle East envoy Jason Greenblatt. But the president had another idea, and, as usual, he went with it. As we were wrapping up lunch, he surprised everyone by saying, "Would anyone like to see the Oval Office?" The ambassadors were already over the moon with the access they had been given to the president. This was total icing on the cake.

It was classic Trump—the Trump that doesn't always come across on television. He was charming and funny and he immediately disarmed the ambassadors. He posed with every one of them and their wives for pictures in front of the Resolute Desk. If I had to guess, I would say none of the ambassadors came to Washington that day with a particularly high opinion of the president. But they all left giddy about the time they had spent with him. And they all wanted their pictures from the Oval Office—the Russian ambassador more than anybody.

I thought the trip was a huge success. We had shown we meant business at the United Nations. But others in Washington didn't share my view of the trip. A story appeared in *The New York Times* a few days later announcing that the State Department would now insist on pre-clearing my remarks at the United Nations. I had always had my staff share my remarks with the State Department before I delivered them. And we had always taken any factual changes they had to offer. But pre-clearance was another thing entirely.

The story quoted an email supposedly sent to my staff from State declaring that remarks on Syria, Iran, the Palestinian-Israeli conflict, and North Korea had to be pre-cleared. It was a phony story. Nobody on my staff had seen any such email from the State Department. It was a clumsy effort, but the message and the timing of the story was unmistakable. Someone in Washington wanted me on a shorter leash. I returned to New York thankful I was escaping the backbiting, ego-obsessed culture of Washington, D.C. Needless to say, we didn't change our approach to speeches or anything else.

7

Maximum Pressure

Otto Warmbier had been in what the doctors called a state of "unresponsive wakefulness" for almost a year when I came to the United Nations. All I knew then about Otto was what most Americans knew: He was a twenty-one-year-old college student on a tour of North Korea when he was arrested and held hostage in January 2016. His "crime" was trying to take a propaganda poster from a hotel in Pyongyang. His forced confession appeared on North Korean state television in March. Then, at his "trial" in April, he was sentenced to fifteen years of hard labor. After that, the world didn't hear much about Otto Warmbier.

It wasn't until June 2017 that the North Koreans finally admitted that Otto was in an unconscious state. The State Department under President Obama had told the Warmbier family to stay quiet and let them handle it. The department said discreet diplomacy provided the best chance to get their son home. But Otto did not come home for seventeen months. Things changed when President

Trump heard about Otto's condition. He pushed hard for Otto to be returned to America and his family. Just days after learning about his condition, the State Department secretly sent a plane to Pyongyang and successfully rescued Otto. But when he finally arrived home to Cincinnati on June 13, his parents were not prepared for what they saw.

As he ascended the stairs of the airplane that brought Otto home, his father, Fred Warmbier, described hearing what he called an "inhuman" sound. It was his son. He was strapped to a gurney, his head shaved, wailing incoherently. When Fred leaned in to hug him, Otto showed no sign of recognition. His eyes were open but unseeing. He was deaf. This was Fred's son, but it wasn't his son. The tall, smart, likable boy, the athlete, gifted student, and prom king, was gone. Otto died six days after returning home.

Otto Warmbier put a human face on a dictatorship in North Korea that will go down as one of the most repressive and barbaric in human history. Kim Jong Un inherited his absolute control of North Korea from his father, who had inherited it from his father. Kim was young when he became dictator. He consolidated his power by executing his competitors, including family members. Estimates are that he had well over 300 people killed in his first six years as leader. No "offense" was too small. Kim reportedly executed one of his generals with an anti-aircraft gun for falling asleep in a meeting.

The Kim regime enforces absolute control through complete surveillance and tight restrictions on the North Korean people's contact with the outside world. Cell phone coverage is blocked and North Korea's version of the internet is a closed network that few people are allowed to use. The regime uses food as a tool of political control, awarding those who comply and deliberately starving those who don't. It operates a system of prison camps that torture, starve, and work to death people who say the wrong things or read the wrong books or media. The United Nations found that hundreds of thousands of North Koreans have died in these camps during the Kim dictatorship. Women are subjected to forced abortion and their babies to infanticide. Escapees report that having a Bible is punishable by imprisonment in the camps.

On top of being the world's worst, most systematic violator of human rights, the North Korean regime posed the number-one security threat to the United States in 2017. North Koreans are taught from childhood to hate and fear the United States. They have long dreamed of uniting the Korean Peninsula under North Korea's control and see the United States as a major obstacle to this. To ensure the dictatorship's survival, the Kim regime has long pursued nuclear weapons, but under Kim Jong Un the country's efforts to develop a long-range missile capable of carrying a nuclear warhead into U.S. territory accelerated alarmingly.

Between February and the end of May in 2017, the North Koreans conducted nine illegal ballistic-missile launches. On July 4—not at all coincidentally on Independence Day—the North Korean regime launched an intercontinental ballistic missile (ICBM) capable of reaching Alaska. In August, they launched two ICBMs. One flew directly over Japan, threatening the mainland of Japan, as well as American, South Korean, and Japanese bases throughout Asia. In September, they exploded their most powerful nuclear weapon to date, a hydrogen bomb.

In November, the North Korean regime launched an intercontinental ballistic missile capable of hitting anywhere in the United States. With that, the Kim regime declared itself a nuclear power.

The North Koreans had openly stated that their missiles were intended to deliver nuclear weapons to strike cities in the United States, South Korea, and Japan. Now they unquestionably had the capacity to do so. It was as dangerous a situation as the United States had encountered in years. The air in Washington and New York was full of a constant, unsettling fear—that we were only one provocation away from a terrible conflict.

THE TRUMP ADMINISTRATION'S APPROACH TO North Korea, more than any other country except Iran, represented a fundamental break from the past. For over twenty years, both Republican and Democratic presidents had tried various strategies to stop the regime's nuclear and ballistic-missile programs. These strategies consisted mostly of trying to bribe Pyongyang into good behavior. What was worse, these bribes were not conditional. North Korea had to do nothing but promise to change its behavior in order to receive aid from the United States. Only after the regime had gotten what it wanted did the United States realize that their promises would not be kept.

The Trump administration took a fundamentally different approach. The policy of "strategic patience" proclaimed by President Obama was over. We would no longer rely on a policy of appeasement to try to persuade the Kim regime to give up its nuclear program. U.S. presidents had been kicking the can down the road on North Korea for years. There was no longer any road to kick the can down.

The new policy came to be called the "maximum pressure" campaign. Part of the new policy was military preparedness. Although we were committed to finding a diplomatic solution, the president never took the possibility of military action off the table. We would deliver a devastating blow if North Korea used its missiles against the United States or our allies. And we made sure the North Koreans knew it.

We also exerted pressure through diplomacy, encouraging other nations to cut off political and trade ties with North Korea.

At the center of the pressure campaign was sanctioning the North Korean regime—making Kim Jong Un and the ruling elite "bleed" until they finally agreed to serious, unconditional negotiations that would ultimately eliminate their nuclear weapons. After the North Koreans launched their first ICBM capable of reaching the United States on July 4, we began work at the United Nations on the first of what would be three sanctions packages.

When I took to the Security Council chamber to announce our new, more aggressive approach, Otto Warmbier was very much on my mind. It was less than a month since he had come home to die. I spoke directly to the American people about the unique evil of the North Korean regime. Americans had seen how barbarically the North Koreans had treated Otto. It was a sign to all of us that the Kim regime was capable of barbaric acts on a much larger scale.

"To Americans, the death of one innocent person can be as powerful as the death of millions," I told the Security Council. "Because all men and women are created in God's image, depravity toward one is a sure sign of willingness to do much more harm."

In the coming days, we will bring before the Security Council a resolution that raises the international response in a way that is proportionate to North Korea's new escalation. I will not detail that resolution here today, but the options are all known to us.

If we are unified, the international community can cut off the major sources of hard currency to the North Korean regime. We can restrict the flow of oil to their military and their weapons programs. We can increase air and maritime restrictions. We can hold senior regime officials accountable.

There was no time to waste. The missile launches were ongoing, and the regime's capabilities were increasing with each launch. We had to light a fire under a bureaucracy that was used to taking months to prepare a sanctions resolution, when we only had days.

The other immediate hurdle was China. The Chinese were North Korea's largest trading partner and top political ally. China could stop North Korean sanctions dead in their tracks in two important ways. First, the Chinese could veto any sanctions resolution in the Security Council. And, second, no sanctions package could be enforced without the active cooperation of China. Ninety percent of trade with North Korea was from China. If the Chinese chose not to honor or to evade the sanctions, the whole exercise would be a waste of time.

In short, negotiating North Korean sanctions in the Security Council was effectively a bilateral negotiation with the Chinese.

I got some good advice from an old China hand on how to approach this. Shortly after I came to New York, former secretary of state Henry Kissinger reached out to me. I was new in town and new to international diplomacy. It was a generous and kind thing to do.

Dr. Kissinger and I began to have regular lunches. One of the best pieces of advice he gave me was this: Put yourself in your adversary's shoes. Understand what he wants and use that to guide your negotiation. You don't have to agree with him—most times you won't. But you have to understand his motivations. You have to understand where he's coming from.

This advice didn't apply only to China, but I put it to good use in our negotiations. There was one thing I knew the Chinese feared above all else: the fall of the Kim regime in North Korea. North Koreans had only known rule by the Kim dynasty. And the Kims had structured the entire North Korean economic and security state around rewarding those who pledged total allegiance to them and brutally punishing those who didn't. The fall of Kim Jong Un's government could mean a massive exodus of poor, desperate North Koreans into China. It could also mean the unification of the Korean Peninsula under a pro-Western government. The stakes for China were very high.

My approach was direct with the Chinese ambassador: I know your concerns about North Koreans fleeing to your country. We know you don't want war with North Korea. This sanctions package will not cause either of those to happen, I said. Kim Jong Un was on an unsustainable path. Left unchecked, he would force an outcome that neither the United States nor China wanted.

I assured the Chinese delegation that I was trying to keep the situation from getting out of hand. So let's work together, I said. When they didn't respond, I told them that doing nothing was not an option. The United States was going to do something. If China wasn't with us, everyone was going to wonder why. But if China decided to stand with us against the North Koreans, we would get the rest of the Security Council on board to give them cover.

We were initially far apart, but the United States kept pushing. Eventually we agreed on a set of sanctions that directly targeted North Korea's export market and therefore the hard currency the country needed to fund its nuclear program. The sanctions banned

North Korea's exports of coal, iron, and seafood, among other things, amounting to one-third of its exports and hard currency.

It was the single largest set of sanctions ever leveled against the North Koreans—the most stringent set of worldwide sanctions on *any country* in a generation. Once China and the United States had agreed on the resolution, support on the Security Council was unanimous, except for one member. You can be sure of it every time: the Russians.

Once again they dug in their heels. They hadn't been consulted on the sanctions, they said, and they wouldn't agree to them. They had the power to torpedo the resolution with their veto. But by then I'd learned a thing or two about dealing with the Russians. We had deliberately waited to find agreement with the Chinese because we anticipated the Russian obstructionism. I put it to them plainly. They were isolated in their opposition to the resolution.

"If you are happy with North Korea's actions, veto it. If you want to be a friend to North Korea, veto it," I said announcing the resolution. "If you choose to do that, we will go our own path. But it makes no sense not to join together on this threat against North Korea. They have not had any care for Russia or China in this, they have not listened to anything that you say.

"To sit there and oppose sanctions, or to sit there and go in defiance of this resolution, means you're holding hands with Kim Jong Un."

It worked. With the Chinese having agreed to join us, the Russians did not want to be the world's only defender of North Korea. The sanctions were passed unanimously on August 5, 2017. It was, at last, a real triumph. The sanctions would cut deep and give the North Korean leaders a taste of the deprivation they were inflicting on the North Korea people. No other organization but the United Nations could have imposed sanctions of this seriousness and scope.

No other organization could bring the world together, if only for a moment, to take action against the North Korean regime. Some Security Council members wanted to hold the vote in a secret session, but we insisted on an open debate. It was a historic day in the Security Council. We were united for the first time against a growing, global menace. Even if it made the Russians uncomfortable, the world needed to know.

But we weren't kidding ourselves. Over the course of the summer, the North Korean missile tests continued, improving in range.* And as they did, President Trump and the Kim regime ramped up their rhetoric. In early August, the president infamously said that any more threats from North Korea would be "met with fire, fury, and frankly power the likes of which this world has never seen before." For the first time, a U.S. president was matching the North Koreans blow for blow. Even some of his rhetoric sounded the same.

The president's provocative words were criticized by many, but they actually helped me in my part of the "maximum pressure" strategy. After North Korea exploded a hydrogen bomb in early September, we were back at the negotiation table to level another set of sanctions. The rhetoric flying back and forth between Washington and Pyongyang had heightened tensions in the second round of negotiations. We used it to our advantage.

"Tell them you just talked to the president," President Trump said to me. "Tell them every option is on the table. Make them think I'm crazy."

It was what Henry Kissinger called the "madman theory." I assured the Chinese that I understood their fear. They didn't want a

*https://www.washingtonpost.com/news/worldviews/wp/2017/12/21/what-made -north-koreas-weapons-programs-so-much-scarier-in-2017/; http://abcnews.go.com /International/north-korean-missile-test-year/story?id=46592733

crisis on the peninsula. I can help you avoid that, I said. But this is what I can't help you with: I can't promise you the president won't act on his own if you don't work with us.

President Trump was on board with the act. In his tweets, he was communicating directly to Kim Jong Un. Later, when asked about direct talks with the dictator himself, the president didn't rule them out.

"As far as the risk of dealing with a madman is concerned," he said, "that's his problem, not mine."

The goal of the second set of sanctions was no longer to get the North Koreans to the negotiating table. It was to starve the regime of the revenue it needed to finance its nuclear and ballistic-missile programs. The new sanctions targeted North Korea's oil imports, cutting them by 30 percent. And it banned more of the nation's exports. In total, more than 90 percent of North Korea's exports were now banned by sanctions.

"Previous efforts to bring North Korea to the negotiating table have failed. They have repeatedly walked back every commitment they have made," I told the Security Council after the sanctions passed. "Today the Security Council has acted in a different way. Today we are attempting to take the future of the North Korean nuclear program out of the hands of its outlaw regime.

"We're done trying to prod the regime to do the right thing. We are now acting to stop it from having the ability to continue doing the wrong thing."

Because so much ground had been covered in the first set of sanctions, the second set was less sweeping than the first. Even so, Secretary Tillerson expressed doubt that we would ever get the sanctions past the Russians and the Chinese. It wasn't easy. We had to give some ground, but once again we won unanimous Security

Council approval for the sanctions. Building on the first package, it was once again the toughest set of sanctions ever leveled on the North Korean regime.

EVERY YEAR AT THE OPENING of the UN General Assembly in September, New York has what is called "high-level week." This is when world leaders come to New York to address the General Assembly and meet with their counterparts. It's a busy, chaotic, crowded time. You can't get a hotel room. You can't get a cab. The security around UN Headquarters is almost impossible to navigate. High-level week 2017 would be when Donald Trump made his first trip to the United Nations as president.

I called the president the week before high-level week to make sure he was all set to come up to New York. I was a little concerned. He didn't know the UN. Speaking to the General Assembly was a different dynamic than he was used to. I wanted him to understand that it was going to be difficult for him to read the room. It was formal, even stiff. People weren't going to clap.

I said, "Just think of it like church. It's going to be like church."

He said he got it.

Later, just a couple days before he would appear at the UN, the president sent me his speech to get my opinion. I said I thought it was fantastic, and it was.

"What do you think of this?" the president asked me. "What do you think of me calling Kim Jong Un 'Little Rocket Man' in the General Assembly?"

"Remember when I said this was going to be like church?" I answered. "This is a very serious crowd. That's not something they would be used to hearing."

The president protested.

"I tweeted it this morning and it's killing on Twitter," he said.

He was the president. If he wanted to do it, he was going to do it.

"It's okay if you want to do it, just know that I don't know what kind of reaction you're going to get," I said.

When it came time for the president's speech, the General Assembly room was packed. As he began to speak you could have heard a pin drop. There was total silence in the room. I noticed that the North Korean delegation was sitting in the front row, directly in front of the president. I held my breath as he got to the part of his speech that addressed North Korea's nuclear threat.

"The United States has great strength and patience, but if it is forced to defend itself or its allies, we will have no choice but to totally destroy North Korea," he said.

"Rocket Man is on a suicide mission for himself and for his regime."

I watched the delegates look at each other. Some laughed. Some murmured. Others had to wait for the foreign language translation before they reacted. It created a kind of ripple effect in the room. Everyone was completely taken aback. But they also relaxed a little bit.

The media was scandalized, of course. So were some of the government officials: The Swedish foreign minister said it was "the wrong speech, at the wrong time, to the wrong audience." But a funny thing happened afterward. I had a meeting later that day with the president of Uganda, Yoweri Museveni. He's in his seventies and a veteran of numerous conflicts, including the rebellion that toppled the Ugandan dictator Idi Amin. We talked about the speech, and he said, "So what are we going to do about Little

Rocket Man?" It was another case of Trump fascinating and disarming international leaders.

A COUPLE MONTHS LATER, ON November 29, "Rocket Man" upped the ante. North Korea launched a missile that could hit anywhere in the United States.* Our intelligence confirmed that the missile flew higher and farther than any North Korean missile had before. We had to respond, but it was clear that this was going to be the most difficult negotiation yet. Russia was pushing back even harder than before. And the Chinese were much more cautious. By this point, the North Korean regime was mad, and its friends in Russia and China were feeling its wrath.

Once again we targeted refined petroleum products going into North Korea. Our proposed sanctions would cut by 89 percent the Kim regime's ability to import products like gas and diesel.

Another major source of revenue for North Korea is the workers it sends abroad, virtual slaves whose earnings are heavily taxed by the North Korean government. We gave the countries who host these workers—Russia chief among them—twenty-four months to expel them all. Our proposal also took the ban on North Korean exports from 90 percent to virtually everything. We were rapidly approaching the point where we could do no more to isolate the Kim regime.

The Chinese have a metaphor for their relationship with North Korea. It translates roughly as, "If the lips are gone the teeth will be cold." North Korea is a kind of geographic security buffer for China. And although they had worked commendably to achieve Security

---

*https://www.cfr.org/backgrounder/north-koreas-military-capabilities; https://missilethreat.csis.org/missile/hwasong-14/

Council unity on North Korea sanctions so far, by the third round, the Chinese were starting to balk. Their worst-case scenario—the fall of the Kim regime leaving refugees and chaos in its wake—was always on their mind. They had to balance their desire to rein in Kim Jong Un's nuclear capacity with their desire to see him stay in power.

To ratchet up the pressure on China, we held a Security Council session in December to highlight the horrific human rights abuses in North Korea, particularly what happens to escaping North Koreans who are caught in China and sent back home.

The Chinese fought convening the meeting, and for good reason. We brought in two North Korean women who had successfully escaped after having been caught by the Chinese and forcibly sent back to North Korea. The stories they told were blood-curdling. One woman was sent back to North Korea by the Chinese three times before she finally escaped. The punishment reserved for these escapees, who are mostly women, is severe. The woman told of being forced to abort without anesthesia the child she conceived in China. At one prison camp, the bodies of the inmates who had starved to death were fed to the guard dogs. Both women told of being raped, starved, and forced into hard labor.

"These are real stories of real people. These things happened," I told my colleagues. "They should motivate us to do more."

China was being more stubborn than ever. But it was clear it took the sanctions negotiations seriously. At one point, the Chinese sent in a high-level delegation from Beijing to negotiate with us. We met in our conference room.

The Chinese had an annoying way of coming into a meeting and completely monopolizing the conversation. Their attitude was arrogant. They would read long statements without any give-and-take. They would do this as a way to set the terms of further discussions, not expecting their initial long-winded speech to be the end of the talks. Their high-level delegation started to do exactly this. They spent twenty minutes talking just to say something very simple— that they weren't going to agree to our sanctions proposal.

I wasn't going to be rude, but I also was not going to accept their tactic. They were wasting my time and everyone else's time.

"I get what you're trying to do," I said. "We have an issue, but you apparently don't want to solve it. I'm sorry you took such a long flight from Beijing to come here, because we don't have anything more to discuss. I will make sure I tell the president."

I thanked them for their time, got my things, and walked out of the room to the visible panic of the staff on both sides.

By the next day, we were talking again. And when the sanctions passed three days before Christmas, I made sure to single out the Chinese delegation for thanks. It was another milestone set of sanctions. It had been a very long time since such unanimity was achieved at the UN to isolate a member state so thoroughly. If the words "maximum pressure" had any meaning, we had achieved it.

DURING THIS SAME TIME I was developing a relationship with Fred and Cindy Warmbier. As a mom, I hurt for them. We met several times. Sometimes he was the stronger one, sometimes she was. It was always painful. But they were very grateful about what we had done to bring Otto home and to take on the Kim regime. Even though Otto had died, they were thankful that we had been loud about their son, that we had stood up in public to advocate for him in the way the Obama administration never did.

I met with a number of the families of hostages during my time at the UN. The Warmbiers were a lesson for me. After meeting them, I always told other families to speak up for their loved ones. Be loud, I said, because the countries holding them get embarrassed when you expose them. It's not a moral response on their part, it's a tactical one. Just like the North Koreans, they don't want U.S. hostages to die in their custody. The Kim regime only sent Otto home because they knew he was going to die. The great tragedy of the whole situation is that the United States didn't begin to speak out about Otto until it was too late.

As moms, Cindy and I bonded especially closely. Cindy said she pulled her strength from me. If I could go out and face the North Koreans in the Security Council, she said, she knew she could do more to get justice for Otto. After his death, Otto's friends got tattoos of a design that spelled his name. Otto's high school art teacher turned the design into a pendant for a necklace that Cindy and Fred gave to me. From then on, whenever I spoke about North Korea I wore it.

The Warmbiers also developed a relationship with President Trump. They were his guests at his 2018 State of the Union Address. They rose to a standing ovation in the gallery of the House Chamber when President Trump mentioned Otto's treatment by the North Korean regime. But as President Trump's rhetoric warmed toward Kim Jong Un, Fred and Cindy had an understandably hard time. It was difficult for them to separate the murder of their son from the larger effort to denuclearize North Korea. They were careful not to say anything in public, but they let me know when they thought their son's memory was being disrespected.

When the White House came out with a commemorative coin in advance of President Trump's first summit meeting with Kim Jong Un in Singapore in June 2018, Cindy texted me that she was deeply upset. She felt it was a glorification of the man she held responsible for her son's death. She called me, just to rant. I listened to her. It was the least I could do.

Then, after the second summit in Hanoi in February 2019, President Trump appeared to absolve Kim from any responsibility for Otto's death.

"I don't believe he would have allowed that to happen," the president said in a post-summit news conference. "He tells me he didn't know about it, and I take him at his word."

I knew what the president was doing. He was trying to communicate with Kim without understanding how his words would be taken by the American people and the Warmbier family. I don't believe he meant any ill will. Still, I knew how Fred and Cindy would take his remarks. I needed to respond before they did.

So I tweeted:

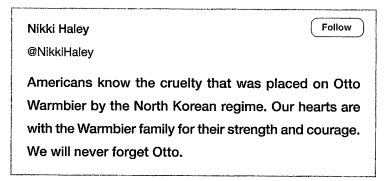

Nikki Haley
@NikkiHaley   Follow

Americans know the cruelty that was placed on Otto Warmbier by the North Korean regime. Our hearts are with the Warmbier family for their strength and courage. We will never forget Otto.

The president walked back his comment about Kim—some. More important, though, in the long term, is that he walked away from the negotiating table in Hanoi rather than give in to the regime's demands that the sanctions be lifted before North Korea took concrete, irreversible steps toward denuclearization. He put the brakes on the developing belief that the "maximum pressure" campaign had been replaced by a "maximum flattery" campaign.

In the end, whether Kim Jong Un will ever end North Korea's development of a deliverable nuclear weapon is an open question. What there is no question about is that we are in a better place in 2019 than we were in 2016 and 2017—not just in terms of North Korea's behavior, but in terms of the strength of United States policy.

The sanctions we passed at the UN were a huge departure from previous administrations' policies toward North Korea. Instead of trying to placate the North Korean dictator, we have set up a system of massive international repercussions for his dangerous behavior. Not only did the sanctions bring the regime to the negotiating table, they have undeniably made North Korea weaker and less able to finance the expansion of its military machine. Kim is demonstrably less able to threaten America and the world. And as long as the sanctions remain, and are enforced, he will not become more so.

What happens next, we cannot know. It's up to the North Korean regime to decide if it wants to live with the UN sanctions in order to cling to its nuclear program. The North Koreans live in a system designed to make sure those who toe the party line are rewarded with a higher standard of living. Sanctions will continue to erode this system of political bribery. But the process of ending the North Korean nuclear threat will be a long one.

Until then, we miss Otto. We will never forget Otto.

8

Changing the Culture

On February 19, 2017, I attended my first Security Council session entitled, innocently enough, "Consultations on the Situation in the Middle East." All of us have heard the stories of unfairness and dysfunction at the United Nations. We've heard about the anti-Israel bias. I was prepared for some of that when I walked into this meeting. I was not prepared for how bad it was.

Just to put things in perspective, at the time the Security Council held its monthly meeting devoted to "the situation in the Middle East," the Syrian regime was using chemical weapons on its own people as part of its bloody civil war. Hezbollah was building up an illegal war arsenal in Lebanon. Hamas had just chosen a terrorist as the leader of its "government" in Gaza—a terrorist who had been sentenced to four life terms in Israel for murder and kidnapping. Linking it all together was Iran, which was not only supporting Assad, Hezbollah, and Hamas, but was also testing ballistic missiles, in violation of the spirit of the nuclear agreement and the letter of UN Security Council resolutions.

Iran was and is the very definition of a Middle East regional threat. And yet the meeting of the Security Council that day was devoted to one country: Israel.

It had been that way for decades. In a region full of conflict, the Security Council has a meeting each month whose only purpose is to bash Israel. They call this regular meeting "consultations on the situation in the Middle East," but only Israel and the Palestinians are on the agenda. And only one country is singled out for blame—Israel. It's just one of the symptoms of the United Nations' obsession with the world's only Jewish state. In my time at the UN, I sat in many of these meetings. Each ambassador read prepared statements saying exactly the same thing, over and over, month after month. It was a complete waste of everyone's time.

The whole exercise was tone-deaf—or worse—to the reality of conflict in the Middle East. After that first meeting, I wanted my fellow Americans to know what I had seen. There is a press stakeout area just outside the Security Council. I decided that was the right platform at which to talk about what I had just witnessed.

I mentioned all the current issues confronting the UN in the Middle East—the war in Syria, the illegal missiles in Lebanon, the ongoing terrorism of ISIS—and how the Security Council had just completely ignored them in order to gang up on the only democracy in the region.

"I am new around here, but I understand that's how the Council has operated, month after month, for decades," I said. "I'm here to say the United States will not turn a blind eye to this anymore."

The anti-Israel bias at the UN was so bad that it had actually become part of the culture there. That culture manifests itself in a lot of ugly speeches, but also in more concrete ways. The UN Department of Political Affairs has a division completely devoted to Palestinian affairs. There is no division devoted to North Korean nuclear missiles or to Iran's support for terrorism. Each year, the General Assembly (where the United States has no veto) passes multiple resolutions targeting Israel and very few if any targeting Syria, Iran, North Korea, or other dictatorships.

More important, the culture of anti-Israel bias at the UN makes peace less likely. It sends the false message to the Palestinians that they can achieve their goals by relying on the UN rather than direct negotiations with Israel. And it sends the accurate message to the Israelis that they can never trust the UN. This disproportionate criticism of Israel isn't the path to peace. It is the path to an endless stalemate.

Once again, I wanted to make a clear break with the past. The Obama administration had seen the Israeli-Palestinian conflict almost exclusively in terms of Israeli settlements in the West Bank. When my staff moved into the UN offices at the State Department in Washington, the walls were covered with maps of Israeli settlements, left there by departing Obama officials.

Not only that, the Obama administration tried harder to fit in with the anti-Israel culture at the UN than to challenge it. When the Security Council, under the pretext of condemning the settlements, judged all of Israel's 1967 territorial actions as illegal in Resolution 2334, the Obama administration abstained.

I was determined that the United States would lead once again at the United Nations. Changing the culture at the UN meant calling attention to the real threats we face in the Middle East. For the next two years, at the monthly "situation in the Middle East" meetings, we talked about Iran's illegal weapons transfers to Yemen, its support for terrorism throughout the region, the barbarism of the Assad regime in Syria, Hamas's illegal and diabolical use of human shields, Iraq, ISIS, refugees, and humanitarian crises.

We occasionally talked about Israel. Israel isn't perfect. But that was never our focus. We were determined to respond when we saw our friends bashed and our values demeaned in the Security Council chamber. And we made an impact. The anti-Israel bias still exists; but several other countries followed our lead, and now this monthly session is at least more balanced.

Later, I talked to a meeting of American supporters of Israel about the new approach we were bringing to the UN.

"I wear heels," I said. "It's not for a fashion statement. It's because if I see something wrong, we're going to kick them every single time."

IN THE FIRST MONTHS OF my ambassadorship, it became clear to me that there were sharp divisions among the president's cabinet about the policies he supported. One policy regarded our embassy in Israel. President Trump had made a campaign promise to do what previous presidents had said they supported but never did: move the U.S. embassy from Tel Aviv to Jerusalem.

Jerusalem has been the political, cultural, and spiritual homeland of the Jewish people for thousands of years. They have had no other capital city. In 1995, in recognition of this fact, Congress voted to move our embassy to Jerusalem and to recognize that city as the capital of Israel. Every president since then—Republican and Democrat—expressed support for moving our embassy, but none actually did it. President Trump also supported the move, but he intended to follow through on Congress's action. He was determined to see our embassy in Jerusalem. Planning on how and when to execute the move began early in the administration.

I supported the move. It was simple common sense. Embassies are located in capitals. In virtually every country in the world, the U.S. embassy is located in the host country's capital city. Israel should be no different. Jerusalem was already home to Israel's parliament, president, prime minister, Supreme Court, and many of its ministries.

But others in the cabinet and the White House disagreed. They argued that moving the embassy would set off violence that would damage the peace process, such as it was. But a peace process that is damaged by the simple recognition that Jerusalem is the capital of Israel is not a peace process at all. Still, there was real resistance to recognizing this. One White House official tried to enlist me in convincing the president to back off his promise to move the embassy. I refused, because I wanted the president to go ahead with it.

In every meeting of the president's cabinet and national security advisors, there was a faction that seemed to think they, not the president, should make the final decision when it came to policy. When the National Security Council met to consider moving the embassy in Israel, the members of this faction were out in force. They implied in every way that if the president did this, the sky would fall. They thought they could team up and spin the president—and they tried. Some, like Secretary of State Tillerson, seemed to be thinking primarily about how the decision would affect their reputations. He declared in the middle of the meeting that he wanted to be on record opposing the move.

Around the world, most who opposed moving the embassy didn't make an argument against it. They issued threats. Some came from the usual sources. Hamas called the move a "declaration of war" that "means the official announcement of the end of the peace process." The leader of Al-Qaeda, Ayman al-Zawahiri, called for followers to escalate "jihad" against the United States.

Just about everyone predicted massive violence. Western leaders were less colorful than Hamas, but their message was the same. UN secretary-general António Guterres said the decision resulted in "a moment of great anxiety." German chancellor Angela Merkel declared she did not support the move. French president Emmanuel Macron called it "regrettable." British prime minister Theresa May said it was "unhelpful in terms of prospects for peace in the region."

At the critical National Security Council meeting with the president on the Jerusalem embassy decision, myself, Vice President Pence, and Ambassador David Friedman spoke out in favor of the move. Everyone else either opposed it or expressed strong reservations. The president made the decision.

On December 6, President Trump announced that the United States would "acknowledge the obvious: that Jerusalem is Israel's capital." He directed the State Department to begin the process of moving the U.S. embassy from Tel Aviv to Jerusalem. But his announcement contained a critical clarification. He made it clear that the decision did not mean the United States was any less committed to achieving a peace agreement acceptable to both Israel and the Palestinians. The United States was also not taking a position on disputed territories, including the future boundaries of Jerusalem itself. These issues were still left for the parties to resolve themselves.

The president made his announcement on a Wednesday. Friday is typically the day protests occur in most Middle Eastern countries, when the mosques empty out after Friday prayer. But on the next Friday, December 8, the promised "third intifada"—or Palestinian uprising against Israel—did not occur. The violence and chaos on the Arab street, which had been the chief argument against moving the embassy to Jerusalem, did not materialize. The sky did not fall. It was still up there.

For many, the lack of a violent response seemed to be a disappointment. The United Nations, having failed to see the result it wanted from the people, tried to produce it itself. The Security Council called an emergency session. A resolution condemning the decision to move our embassy was quickly drafted. I got my back up. The United States is a sovereign nation. Where we put our embassies is our decision. The Security Council had no business condemning us for exercising our sovereign rights.

"I suspect very few Member States would welcome Security Council pronouncements about their sovereign decisions," I told the council. "And I can think of some who should fear it."

But we were outvoted. We were opposed by every other member of the council. I was left with no choice. For the first time as U.S. ambassador, I exercised our veto power over the resolution. But first I offered this warning:

"What we witnessed here today in the Security Council is an insult," I said. "It won't be forgotten. It's one more example of the United Nations doing more harm than good in addressing the Israeli-Palestinian conflict."

It was one of my proudest moments.

We vetoed the resolution in the Security Council, but the UN was not about to give up on its anti-Israel, anti-American narrative. The General Assembly quickly drafted a resolution condemning the president's action. A vote was called for December 21, 2017. We knew what was coming. We had been on the losing side of lopsided General Assembly votes, particularly on Israel, many times.

Like virtually everything the General Assembly does, this vote was just symbolic. The United States was going to move its embassy, regardless of what the UN said.

But there would be consequences of the vote nonetheless. I spelled them out to the General Assembly in the minutes before the vote.

"The United States will remember this day in which it was singled out for attack in the General Assembly for the very act of exercising our right as a sovereign nation," I said.

"We will remember it when we are called upon to once again make the world's largest contribution to the United Nations. And we will remember it when so many countries come calling on us, as they so often do, to pay even more and to use our influence for their benefit."

The General Assembly went on to vote 128–9 to condemn the United States' decision to move its embassy to Jerusalem. A record thirty-five countries chose not to vote. I announced that the U.S. mission would host a party to thank all forty-four countries who declined to oppose the U.S. position.

I was grateful to the nine countries who took the courageous position to stand with us, but I was equally appreciative of the thirty-five countries who refused to vote against the United States.

I always said we would be "taking names," and that goes both ways—taking the names of those who work against us, but also taking the names of those who stand with us.

I took the opportunity to show our gratitude by hosting a thank-you reception for the forty-four countries who showed friendship to us that day. They deserved to know that we noticed and appreciated them. They all showed up.

In the end, the Jerusalem embassy vote was not a complete waste of time. It led us to dive deeper into just exactly what the American people were getting for their investments in both the UN and foreign aid. My staff in New York compiled the data on how often countries voted with us at the UN compared to how much foreign aid we sent them. How a country votes at the UN shouldn't be the only factor in our foreign aid decisions, but it should certainly be one factor, and the disparity we found was shocking.

One example is South Africa. It receives half a billion dollars in U.S. aid each year, but it votes with us on key issues at the UN just 18 percent of the time. Another example: We give Pakistan more aid than all but a handful of countries. In 2017 the United States gave their military almost $1 billion in aid. Pakistan opposes us at the UN a full 76 percent of the time. What's worse, Pakistan harbors terrorists who go out and try to kill our American soldiers. I brought these findings and others to President Trump. He was outraged. Soon after, he asked Congress to pass legislation ensuring that U.S. foreign aid only goes to promote U.S. interests and U.S. friends.

Humanitarian assistance will always be a priority for the United States. We will always be generous when it comes to saving lives and alleviating suffering. That's who we are as a people. But we should not be the country of mindless handouts. Our focus should be on helping countries that want our help trying to stand on their own two feet, moving from humanitarian assistance to self-reliance. The worst of all possible outcomes is to create permanent reliance on our generosity while bringing countries no closer to supporting our interests.

WHEN IT COMES TO RECEIVING generous U.S. assistance and returning the favor with hostile rhetoric and even more hostile actions toward the United States, the Palestinians stand out. We have done more than any other country to assist the Palestinian people. By far. Since 1994 the United States has given the Palestinians over $5 billion in assistance. During the time I was at the UN, we gave the Palestinian Authority over half a billion dollars in direct and indirect assistance. Still, during that same time, no Palestinian representative was willing to even speak to any U.S. administration representative.

I had heard plenty at the UN about the plight of the Palestinians. I wanted to see it for myself. So I took my first trip to Israel in June of 2017. I visited the Aida Palestinian refugee camp on the West Bank. I saw their living conditions. I saw their classrooms. I saw the nets over the playground that were meant to keep the tear-gas canisters from hitting the children. I spoke to the young girls about the challenges in their lives. Like all young girls, they wanted more than anything for their lives to be normal.

I also saw other things: I saw the anti-Israel graffiti painted along the walls. There were glorified images of Palestinians killing Israeli soldiers. The soldiers were portrayed like demons. There were maps of Palestine in which no Israel existed at all. This was hardly the depiction of a peaceful two-state solution that so many at the UN and in Washington talk about constantly.

It was one of those moments when you think, "No one should have to live like this." I left wishing for a better life for Palestinians. I left praying for safer playgrounds, better health care, and most of all hope. The resentment in the camp was so strong. Reconciliation would be impossible as long as this bad feeling was present and was passed down to future generations.

I came back to New York with hopes of working with the UN agency devoted exclusively to providing services like health care and education to Palestinian refugees. As is typical for the UN, its name is a mouthful: the United Nations Relief and Works Agency for Palestine Refugees in the Near East, or UNRWA.

UNRWA is not like any other refugee agency. It uses a unique definition of "refugee" that has the effect of perpetually increasing the number of Palestinians who are considered refugees. UNRWA passes refugee status on to any and all descendants of the original male Palestinian refugees. It doesn't matter if they've moved to another country or even been granted citizenship there—they are still counted as refugees. Under UNRWA, the number of Palestinian "refugees" has ballooned from seven hundred thousand to five million.

Instead of alleviating dependency, UNRWA *encourages* multigenerational dependency on international aid. Palestinian refugees are funded forever through UNRWA, with no end in sight.

The other, more immediate problem with UNRWA is its role in fueling the resentment I felt in the Palestinian refugee camps. UNRWA promotes the so-called right of return, that is, the alleged right of the ever-growing number of Palestinian refugees to go back to the territory that is now Israel. This is a practical impossibility that is tantamount to the destruction of Israel as the world's only Jewish state. The Arab community understands this very well, as does the Palestinian leadership. And yet, it persists in keeping alive this fantasy that only serves to undermine any chances for peaceful compromise. Through UNRWA, the UN nurtures this obsession that harms the chances of peace.

UNRWA has other problems, too. It has used textbooks that preach violence and hatred toward Jews. Hamas terrorists have built tunnels under UNRWA schools, tunnels that cross under the border with Israel and are used to conduct terror attacks. When my deputy, Jon Lerner, asked the UNRWA commissioner general if he would use readily available geological equipment to detect these tunnels before attacks could occur, he refused. He claimed such a move by UNRWA would be too "provocative" and "political."

We came back from Israel with ideas for how UNRWA could better serve the Palestinian people. But we found that UNRWA didn't want our advice, it just wanted our money. UNRWA is funded almost entirely by voluntary contributions. The United States voluntarily contributed 30 percent of its funding in 2016—that's more than the next two largest donors combined.

The threat constantly wielded by UNRWA and its supporters is that if they didn't get their American money, schools would close. Young Palestinian men would radicalize and turn to terrorism. This was their answer to any serious talk of reform. They used this threat to shut down any attempts to make them cut their bloated bureaucracy and serve the Palestinian people better. It was the same blackmail strategy used when we said we were moving our embassy to Jerusalem. I was tired of it. It didn't advance the cause of peace. It only prolonged the toxic environment brewing in the camps. And it put *our* policy—and the spending of *our* tax dollars—in the hands of people who in no way share our interests.

Armed with our observations from the refugee camps and UNRWA's own shoddy record, we made the case to the State Department that the United States should stop funding UNRWA until it changed its ways. But it was clear from the outset that the bureaucrats in the department did not like the idea—at all. They even used the "How dare we close Palestinian schools?" argument against us. We weren't being told anything from them that we hadn't already heard from UNRWA. So I went and met with President Trump.

Our meeting initially consisted of the president, Chief of Staff John Kelly, and myself. It began well. I made my case for defunding UNRWA until it could be reformed. In the middle of my talk, Kelly left the room for a moment and then returned. Twenty minutes later, Rex Tillerson showed up. By that time, I had convinced the president that withholding the U.S. contribution wouldn't close schools or hurt the Palestinian people, because it would force the countries in the region to step up with more money. As it stood, the assistance that wealthy Arab countries had provided their Palestinian brothers and sisters didn't come close to the United States' yearly almost $400 million contribution to UNRWA. Qatar had contributed $1 million; Kuwait, $5 million; and the United Arab Emirates gave $17 million. Saudi Arabia was the only Arab country that even came close to our funding, with a $148 million contribution to UNRWA. Why should the United States shoulder the burden when the countries in the region wouldn't?

I had a feeling the president would agree with me about the unfairness of this imbalance. When the American people see a group of neighboring countries whose total contributions to the Palestinian people are very small and then they see these countries accuse the United States of not being sufficiently committed to the well-being of Palestinians, the American people lose their patience. And they should.

Rex came into the meeting and sat down. I had to assume Kelly had briefed him on what we'd been talking about, because he automatically began to emphasize how dangerous it would be if we stopped funding UNRWA. There would be riots in the street, he said. There would be threats to Israel (as if there weren't plenty of those already). Most of all, he said, we would upset the Arab countries who were supposed to be essential to helping with the peace process.

I had consulted with the two key administration people working the Israeli-Palestinian peace plan before I met with the president—Jared Kushner and Jason Greenblatt. I had also talked to National Security Advisor McMaster and our U.S. ambassador to Israel, David Friedman. They all agreed with me. But none of them were in the room with me and the president.

Once again, Rex and I began to debate. He went on about the schools closing if the United States acted. I countered that this was the threat UNRWA used every time reform was mentioned. The schools never closed. It was nothing but a bluff. This went on for some time. Rex's scare tactics were starting to work. The president was rethinking his earlier support for my plan. Then, once again, the president told us to resolve our differences and come back and see him.

Chief of Staff Kelly asked me to come to his office to hash out the issue with Rex. I went there and waited. It took about twenty minutes for Kelly and Tillerson to join me. I suspected they had been together coordinating their strategy.

"I have four secretaries of state: you, H. R., Jared, and Rex," said Kelly. "I only need one."

I explained to both of them that I was doing my job, staying in my lane, and never surprising anyone. But I had been stonewalled by the State Department on this multiple times. It was an issue the president deserved to know about. The fact that people at the State Department, including Rex, refused to return my calls was not going to keep me from bringing it up to the president.

Kelly let it slip that he thought making the UN job a cabinet-level position had been a terrible decision by the president. He said he would do everything in his power to ensure that whoever came after me was not a member of the cabinet.

But the fundamental issue wasn't my cabinet status. The issue was that Rex and the president didn't agree on much when it came to policy. Rex was more cautious, more in line with the bureaucracy at the State Department and the foreign-policy establishment. I didn't always agree with the president, either. But I always gave him my opinion honestly and openly. I understood that the buck stopped with him. When he made a decision, I would follow it. Rex struggled with the president's decisions.

Then, when it was clear we weren't going to get anywhere on resolving the UNRWA funding question, the conversation went to a place that took my breath away: challenging the authority of the president himself.

KELLY AND TILLERSON CONFIDED IN me that when they resisted the president, they weren't being insubordinate, they were trying to save the country. It was *their* decisions, not the president's, that were in the best interests of America, they said. The president didn't know what he was doing.

"I don't even think he realizes what the legislative branch is and that members of Congress are elected by the people," Kelly said.

But it wasn't the legislative branch that these men wanted the president to defer to; it was *them*. Tillerson went on to tell me the reason he resisted the president's decisions was because, if he didn't, people would *die*. This was how high the stakes were, he and Kelly told me. We are doing the best we can do to save the country, they said. We need you to work with us and help us do it. This went on for over an hour.

The problem was, I had been in meetings with the president and Tillerson and Kelly. Their idea of "saving the country" was not stopping a president who they thought was somehow unable to do his job. Their idea of "saving the country" was staying in the Iran Nuclear Deal. Staying in the Paris climate agreement. And keeping the U.S. embassy in Tel Aviv, just to name a few. These were major policy decisions in which they disagreed with the president. Their obligation in those situations was to express their disagreement to the president. And if they couldn't change his mind, they needed to carry out his wishes or leave. But that's not what they were doing.

I was so shocked I didn't speak the whole way back to New York. I didn't think the president's advisors were working against him, not directly anyway. But they were definitely working *around him*. They were stalling, distracting, taking matters into their own hands—doing anything they could to resist carrying out his policies. They were heading down a very dangerous path.

Like the president, I am someone who knows how hard it is to run and win an election. Just about everyone in Washington looks in the mirror and thinks they could be president. But winning the support of the American people is no small feat. President Trump, like him or not, won the election. Tillerson and Kelly didn't. That means something important. What they were doing was disloyal to the president. More important, it was disloyal to the American people who elected him.

After the election comes the governing, and I knew something about that, too. With public office comes a great responsibility to serve the people. A governor or a president can't do that if she has people working around her decisions, plotting behind her back, and thinking they are smarter than her. It would have been unbelievably hard for me to govern my state if my chief of staff and members of my cabinet were working to resist me. It's bad, toxic government that doesn't serve anyone.

There were a lot of stories in the media when I was ambassador about people in the president's orbit who were actively working against him. Some, like Kelly and Tillerson, were defying him to supposedly "save the country." But whether they sincerely believed they were doing the right thing or just pushing their personal agendas, these people were dangerous. As H. R. McMaster said after he left the White House, the job of the president's advisors is to provide him with honest policy options and then respect his decisions. What is at stake is not just the policy agenda of Donald Trump. What is at stake is the U.S. Constitution itself, which places executive authority in the president. No disagreement with the president, no matter how heartfelt, justifies undermining the Constitution.

Later, an anonymous senior official in the Trump administration published an op-ed in *The New York Times* announcing that he or she was part of the "resistance" within the administration. The op-ed claimed that the anonymous author was not alone.

"[M]any of the senior officials in [the Trump] administration are working diligently from within to frustrate parts of his agenda and his worst inclinations," it read. The writer pointed to "unsung heroes" like himself or herself who were containing the president's worst impulses by "trying to do what's right even when Donald Trump won't."

I wrote my own op-ed in response. The headline in *The Washington Post* when it ran was, WHEN I CHALLENGE THE PRESIDENT, I DO IT DIRECTLY. MY ANONYMOUS COLLEAGUE SHOULD HAVE, TOO.

I wrote that the anonymous senior official might think he or she is doing a service to America. But, in fact, that person is doing a serious disservice to the president and the country.

"Dissent is as American as apple pie. If you don't like this president, you are free to say so, and people do that quite frequently and loudly," I wrote. "But in the spirit of civility that the anonymous author claims to support, every American should want to see this administration succeed. If it does, it's a win for the American people."

SECRETARY TILLERSON WENT AHEAD AND acted on his own—without the permission of the president—to authorize a $60 million donation to UNRWA, half the $120 million that had previously been pledged. He must have felt he'd won a victory. In fact, he ended up proving my point.

The people in the Palestinian territories did not share Secretary Tillerson's view of the value of our generous contribution. They reacted in protest to this "cut" in their aid. Never mind that our $60 million donation still made us the single largest funder of their schools and their health care that year. Amazingly enough, some UNRWA staffers joined in the protests against the U.S. contribution. It was the very definition of what our assistance should *not* do: encourage dependency and create entitlement instead of self-sufficiency.

Secretary Tillerson was fired in March of 2018. He was replaced as Secretary of State by Mike Pompeo, someone I had worked with on the NSC when he was the Director of Central Intelligence. It was a pleasure and a relief to work with a Secretary of State who actually supported the president's agenda and didn't seek to undermine him. In August, the State Department announced the end of U.S. funding for UNRWA. Despite Rex's dire warnings, no schools closed. Other countries stepped in to fill the funding gap left by the United States. UNRWA stayed funded, but it didn't change. It is still a bloated and corrupt organization that fails the Palestinian people and fails the cause of peace.

In the end, we were only partially successful in changing the culture at the UN. And peace between Israel and the Palestinians is still very much a work in progress. But what we did succeed in doing was leading again. We took our foreign policy back from the bias and the fearmongering that had previously held it hostage. We challenged the conventional wisdom that was getting us nowhere. By showing what American leadership looks like, we opened up new possibilities for progress.

As for myself, I never spoke to Kelly or Tillerson about our conversation again. They understood I was never going to be a part of their effort. And I was determined to continue to do my job. I would be open and honest with the president. And I would try to avoid the drama that was swirling around the White House.

I should have known. Despite my efforts, there was more drama ahead.

9

Beyond the Echo Chamber

It was August of 2017 and I was on a trip very few people supported, to investigate an issue no one wanted to talk about.
President Obama had famously said that the nuclear deal negotiated with Iran "cuts off all of Iran's pathways to a bomb." I was
in Vienna to meet with the officials in charge of verifying Iran's
compliance with the agreement. I was there to find out how we
could be sure that what President Obama said was actually true.

The Obama administration put on a full-court press to convince the American people of the value of the Iran agreement. It
created what it called an "echo chamber" to sell the deal. The "echo
chamber" was a group of loyal academics and think tank experts
to whom the administration fed talking points. The "experts" then
faithfully repeated these talking points to often-clueless reporters,
who wrote them up for the American people.

Even so, it was clear when the agreement was concluded in 2015
that there wasn't support in Congress for the deal with the Iranian

regime. So the Obama administration purposefully did not submit the agreement to the Senate to be ratified as a treaty. It rightly concluded it would have been rejected.

But Congress preserved its power in one significant way, a way that would prove fateful when a new president was elected. It passed a law requiring that every ninety days the president certify certain things about the deal. First, the president must determine that Iran has not violated the terms of the agreement. And, second, the president must confirm that the agreement is in the national security interest of the United States.

We had come to Vienna to determine if, in fact, the new president could continue to do that. It turned out, he couldn't.

BY THE TIME SECRETARY TILLERSON and I had our showdown at Bedminster that August, President Trump had already certified the Iran deal, reluctantly, twice. He had run for president on opposing the deal. He didn't want to certify that it was in the best interests of the American people because he didn't think it was. But most of his cabinet supported continuing the agreement.

I thought the case needed to be properly made to the American public and the international community before we changed the agreement. The offer I made to the president at Bedminster was to do just that.

There was a lot of work to do. In the first six months of the new administration, the conventional wisdom still held that the Iran agreement would "end" Iran's decades-long pursuit of a nuclear weapon. In fact, the deal didn't end Iran's development of a bomb, it just paused it, at best. After ten or, in some cases, fifteen years, the restrictions the agreement placed on the components of a nuclear weapon—the enrichment of uranium, the development of advanced centrifuges and others—began to evaporate. Just ten years after 2015—in other words, very soon—Iran could begin to upgrade its nuclear capabilities in significant ways.

The Obama administration had promised "anytime, anywhere" inspections of sites where Iran had worked on nuclear weapons. But the agreement that was finally reached delivered much, much less. The promised inspections applied only to Iran's "declared" nuclear sites, that is, sites Iran admitted to. For any other locations that were suspected of harboring nuclear activity, the Iranians could deny access to inspectors for up to twenty-four days. They also flatly refused to let inspectors onto military sites. We learned in our meetings with the inspecting officials at the International Atomic Energy Agency (IAEA) in Vienna that there were many such sites.

Most of all, in the first months of the Trump presidency, people still accepted the Obama administration's wrong-to-the-point-of-being-dangerous premise for the deal: that the Iranian regime would deliver on the promises it made.

In fact, the current Iranian regime was created in an act of international lawbreaking and has always existed outside the community of responsible nations. On November 4, 1979, a group of Islamic revolutionary students took over the American embassy in Tehran. They held fifty-two U.S. Marines and diplomats hostage for 444 days. Ever since, the Iranian government's mission has been to spread revolutionary Shia Islam by force.

The focus of Iran's aggression is what it calls the "Great Satan": the United States of America.

An Iranian terrorist proxy group bombed the U.S. embassy in Beirut in 1983. Sixty-three people were killed. Just months later another Iranian proxy bombed the Marine barracks in Beirut. Two

·hundred and forty-one Americans were killed. Throughout the Iraq War, the number-one killer of American troops was improvised explosive devices (IEDs), the deadliest of which were supplied by Iran.*

Today, Iran is the single biggest cause of violence and instability in the Middle East. Pick a terrorist group or a conflict, and Iran is behind it. The regime funds and supports Hezbollah, Hamas, the Palestinian Islamic Jihad, the Taliban, al-Qaeda, Shia militias in Iraq, and Houthi militants·in Yemen. It fuels the bloodshed of the Syrian dictator Assad with arms and men. It provides missiles that are fired into Saudi Arabia from Yemen and into Israel from Gaza. It's hard to find a conflict or a suffering people in the Middle East that does not have Iran's fingerprints on it.

What is perhaps most overlooked in this debate is the Iranian regime's treatment of its own people. Its government denies the basic human rights of Iranians. It forces women to cover, censors the press, and denies freedom of speech, freedom of religion, and access to the internet, among many other things. The Iranian people live in poverty while their government spends billions each year propping up the dictatorship in Syria and supporting terrorist proxies. The regime makes its cronies rich through corruption and sweetheart deals. Huge parts of the economy are owned outright by members of the government and its enforcers. Ordinary Iranians rank a distant second, if they matter at all, to their government.

On top of oppressing its own people and being the world's number-one supporter of terrorism, Iran has for decades worked to develop a nuclear weapon, and lied about it. At multiple points, Iran agreed to stop building secret facilities to develop a nuclear bomb. Each time it

---

*https://www.nytimes.com/2007/02/10/world/middleeast/10weapons.html; https://www.militarytimes.com/news/your-military/2019/04/04/iran-killed-more-us-troops-in-iraq-than-previously-known-pentagon-says/

failed to keep its promise. It has made international agreements and has been subject to UN Security Council resolutions. Each one has been broken or ignored. Iran has consistently claimed its nuclear program exists only for peaceful purposes. But many of its nuclear sites are constructed to be carefully hidden from international inspectors; one was located literally under a mountain. Not only that, Iran has worked relentlessly to develop ballistic missiles capable of carrying a nuclear warhead. None of these things—covert facilities or ballistic missiles—has anything to do with a peaceful nuclear energy program.

This is the government the Obama administration concluded an agreement with in 2015. These are the men it believed would live up to their commitments. No wonder the administration thought it had to work so hard to create support for the deal. But the "echo chamber" campaign wasn't just designed to convince Americans of the legitimacy of the nuclear agreement. It was also designed to make the agreement untouchable once it was concluded. In the language of the financial crisis, the Iran deal was made to be "too big to fail." It was designed to take precedence over all other issues with Iran. It had to be propped up and bailed out by the government no matter how empty its promises were.

The Obama administration tried to create the impression that the Iran deal was too big to fail by portraying it as the only alternative to war. The choice was binary, it told the American people: the Iran deal or war. We are still hearing this argument from supporters of the deal today. In his speech announcing the deal, President Obama could not have made this false choice any clearer.

"Congressional rejection of this deal leaves any U.S. administration that is absolutely committed to preventing Iran from getting a nuclear weapon with one option—another war in the Middle East," the president said.

To make sure that everyone got the point, President Obama told Americans that anyone who failed to support the deal was on the side of the Iranian theocrats, they were just too blinded by their lust for war to realize it.

"It's those hardliners chanting 'Death to America' who have been most opposed to the deal. They're making common cause with the Republican caucus," President Obama said to laughter and applause in a speech at American University.

But it was these same Iranian hard-liners who complained the loudest when we began the process of ending the United States participation in the agreement in the first year of the Trump administration. Sometime between 2015 and 2017, they went from supposedly opposing the Iran deal to indignantly demanding that the United States continue to honor it.

The truth is that this was always a false choice. War is never inevitable. In fact, making terrible deals with the world's most vicious regimes is more likely to lead to war. Demonstrating resolve and strength is more likely to avoid war.

AFTER MY OVAL OFFICE DISCUSSION with the president and the confrontation at Bedminster, my team and I had the go-ahead to make the case against the Iran agreement, but we still faced significant headwinds. Secretary Tillerson argued strenuously that there was no need for us to go to Vienna. He had sent a top deputy to a meeting of the seven parties to the deal in July. No one else needed to verify that Iran was in compliance, he told the president. But we had a different approach than what I suspected Tillerson's deputy had taken. We wanted answers to questions I doubted his people had asked.

The typical question asked about compliance with the Iran deal was, "Is there evidence that Iran is violating it?" The answer from the IAEA, always, was that Iran had not "materially breached" the agreement, that is, the country had not violated it in a significant way. What we wanted to know was different. We intended to ask if there was *reason to believe that Iran was in compliance to begin with.* And what did "compliance" mean? Did it really mean the agreement had cut off "all of Iran's pathways to a bomb"? Or did the agreement simply lay out a series of technical benchmarks meant to give that appearance? Did it make the world any safer to say Iran was abiding by the terms of the nuclear deal?

My team prepared extensively for our meetings with IAEA officials. We consulted with all the experts we could find, including the State Department officials who actually negotiated the agreement. We were prepared to ask detailed questions in Vienna, and we did.

To begin with, Iran had flatly denied that the IAEA could inspect military sites. But we knew these sites were locations where Iran had engaged in nuclear activity in the past. Did the IAEA inspectors know for a fact that no nuclear activity was occurring at these sites? How could they know if Iran refused to allow site inspections?

We had other questions about the crucial issue of exactly how we knew what Iran was up to. The agreement allowed Iran to put off inspections of suspected sites for up to twenty-four days—more than three weeks. What could be done in three weeks to wipe a site clean?

Finally, we asked about Iran's ballistic-missile program. Iran's development of nuclear-capable ballistic missiles had only accelerated since the conclusion of the nuclear agreement. Why had the Iranian regime continued to test ballistic missiles that could carry a nuclear bomb if it had given up its nuclear-weapons program?

We had to pry to get answers, and we asked a lot of follow-up questions. At first, the IAEA officials were welcoming to us. But their warmth deteriorated once they realized we were there to question the basis of their conclusion that Iran was honoring the nuclear agreement. We weren't there to prejudge the answers to our questions. If they had been able to tell us they had timely access to all suspected sites and that the sites had come up clean, our concerns would have been alleviated. If they could have somehow explained Iran's pursuit of ballistic missiles for non-nuclear purposes, we would have left satisfied.

The IAEA leadership and staff are scientists, not politicians or diplomats. They do their jobs well. The problem is not the inspectors. The problem is how the Iran deal itself limited what the inspectors were able to do.

They could not answer our most important questions. We left Vienna more concerned than we were when we arrived.

Thirteen days after I returned from our meeting in Vienna I gave a speech at the American Enterprise Institute (AEI) in Washington, D.C. In the speech I was careful not to try to predict whether the president would certify the Iran agreement the next time he was called on to do so. I didn't know what his decision would be.

I merely asked that we have the debate about Iran we never had when the agreement was concluded. The IAEA chief in Vienna had observed something very interesting to me. He said determining Iranian compliance with the nuclear deal was like a jigsaw puzzle. Looking at just one piece didn't give you the whole picture. You had to put all the pieces together.

I liked and agreed with this metaphor. I had come to the conclusion that the agreement was fatally flawed. But in addition to not cutting òff "all of Iran's pathways to a bomb," as President Obama had promised, it did nothing to address the so-called non-nuclear threats posed by Iran to the region and the world.

As a matter of fact, the nuclear deal encouraged the United States and our European cosignatories to overlook Iran's support for terrorism and war in the Middle East. The deal drew an artificial line between Iran's nuclear development and the rest of its lawless behavior. In effect, it said, "We've made this deal on the nuclear side, so none of the regime's other bad behavior can be allowed to threaten the agreement." The nuclear deal depended on us ignoring what was right in front of our eyes: the true nature of the Iranian regime. American politicians and diplomats were too invested in its success. European countries were too eager for the business opportunities it provided them by lifting sanctions on Iran. In the eyes of many, the Iran deal had truly become "too big to fail."

The result was a national security threat that was increased, not diminished, by the nuclear agreement. "It is this unwillingness to challenge Iranian behavior, for fear of damaging our nuclear agreement, that gets to the heart of the threat the deal poses to our national security," I told the AEI audience.

In addition, the Iran deal was a financial windfall for the fundamentalist Islamic regime. It freed up, by some reports, $100 billion for the government and military, including literally a plane full of cash delivered to Tehran. And all these benefits for Iran were frontloaded: They came first. The regime's supposed compliance with the deal came after.

The Iran deal had been a bet that the regime would change its ways once sanctions were lifted. But that bet had not paid off. I argued that there was a way to address the true security threat posed by Iran if we had the political will to do it. The law passed by Congress mandating presidential certification of the agreement required the president to look beyond the technical aspects of the deal. In other words, narrow "compliance" was not all that mattered.

The president had to conclude that the deal was "vital to the national security interests of the United States." Put simply, the Iranian regime's support for terrorism, its history of lying, its export of weapons to militants, its ballistic-missile program—all the pieces of the jigsaw puzzle—had to be part of his consideration.

The deadline for the next presidential certification of the deal was coming up in October. In the AEI speech, I laid a path forward for the administration and Congress. If the president concluded that the deal was not in the national security interest of the United States and chose not to certify it, the law gave Congress sixty days to consider withdrawing from the deal and reimposing sanctions on Iran. Congress didn't automatically have to take the United States out of the deal. But the American people would, at long last, have a real debate on the Iran agreement.

CRITICS OF MY SPEECH REPEATED the IAEA line about Iran being in technical compliance with the deal and, in doing so, made my point. Iran was wreaking havoc all over the Middle East and zealously pursuing a nuclear-capable missile, but as long as the critics could say Iran was in "compliance" with the deal, that was all that mattered to them. And that was the problem.

In the end, in a decision I applauded, President Trump refused to certify the Iran agreement in October 2017. Instead, he set a deadline of mid-May to determine whether the United States would get out or not. In the following months, however, the case for leaving the deal only grew stronger. Iran's behavior continued to get worse under the shield from scrutiny the deal provided.

In November, Saudi Arabia shot down a missile fired by Iranian-backed militants in Yemen. The missile was headed for an area of Riyadh crowded with government offices. The United Nations released a report about the same time that detailed multiple instances of Iran supplying weapons of war to militant groups, in violation of UN Security Council resolutions. The report provided devastating evidence of missiles, conventional arms—even explosive boats that could blow six-foot holes in the hulls of ships—that came from Iran and were being used by militants in Yemen.

To build on the UN report, we unclassified physical evidence of Iranian missiles and other weapons that had been transferred to Yemen and used by the Houthis to target civilians. We put the evidence on display in a warehouse in Washington, D.C., and invited the UN Security Council, Congress, and the press to see it. When President Trump declined to certify the Iran agreement, he said we were now going to focus on *all* the regime's destabilizing behavior. This was a part of that new approach.

I was in Washington to unveil the display before the press.

"As you know, we do not often declassify this type of military equipment recovered from these attacks," I said. "But today we are taking the extraordinary step of presenting it here in an open setting. We did this for a single, urgent purpose: because the Iranian regime cannot be allowed to engage in its lawless behavior any longer."

The collection included the recovered pieces of yet another Iranian missile fired by Yemeni militants into Saudi Arabia. The missile's intended target was the civilian airport in Riyadh.

"Just imagine if this missile had been launched at Dulles Airport or JFK, or the airports in Paris, London, or Berlin," I told the opening-day crowd. "That's what we're talking about here. That's what Iran is actively supporting."

In January came an even more persuasive sign that Iran's be-havior was getting worse, not better. Protests broke out in over seventy-nine separate locations in Iran. The Iranian people took to the streets in a show of strength not seen since the regime was ac-cused of stealing the elections in 2009. The focus of the people's anger was the economy and their government putting its support of terrorists and dictators over their well-being. The UN had cal-culated that the Iranian regime was spending at least $6 billion a year propping up Assad in Syria. The protestors chanted, "Let go of Syria!" And "Think of us!" It was a clear sign that the billions of dollars that poured into Iran as the result of the nuclear agreement had not been spent to benefit the Iranian people. The money had gone to business as usual: fomenting conflict in the region and sup-porting terrorism throughout the world.

On May 8, 2018, President Trump announced the United States was withdrawing from the Iran Nuclear Deal. The reaction of the defenders of the deal was telling. Few attempted to rebut the administration's critique. Instead, there was immediate, fierce criticism that the U.S. withdrawal put us on the wrong side of our European allies.

I didn't understand this response. The United States had made the case that Iran was a security threat to Europe every bit as much, or more, than it was to the United States. Between the president decertifying the deal and our withdrawal, we went to the Euro-peans again and again, saying we would stay in the deal if they would work with us to address its flaws. We could justify staying in the agreement if they agreed to join us in addressing Iran's missile launches and foreign interference. Our offers were never accepted.

On the day President Trump announced we were leaving the deal, the British, French, and Germans announced they were staying in. But the reasons they offered were not substantive. They boiled down to little more than a fierce protection of the status quo. Just as in the United States, there were European officials whose reputations were invested in the success of the agreement. Some even seemed to lose sight of what they were accountable for, the agreement or the security of their people.

Supporters of the deal argue that the Trump administration set out to destroy the Iran deal out of a desire to undo President Obama's singular foreign-policy initiative. The truth is, there was so much support for the deal in President Trump's cabinet—not to mention virtually unanimous support among the foreign-policy establishment—that the easy thing to do would have been to stay in the deal. We could have agreed with our critics and continued to engage in the dangerous self-deception that technical compliance with the nuclear agreement meant the Iranian regime was no longer a threat. We could have done that and hoped for the best. That would have been the "political" path, but it would not have been the responsible path.

As I write this, the Iranian regime has begun enriching uranium beyond the level permitted in the agreement. It is seizing international ships in the critical Strait of Hormuz. This is a not-so-veiled attempt to get our European friends to stay in the agreement and maybe provide help evading U.S. sanctions. Most of all, it is a reflection of the Iranian leaders' intentions all along. They are not interested in ending their nuclear program. They are interested in using it to blackmail the United States and the world. All signs point to desperation on Iran's part, as its economy crumbles under the weight of U.S. sanctions. And with each additional act of aggression, it validates the president's decision to withdraw from what was a terrible deal.

JUST DAYS BEFORE I LEFT for Vienna, something happened that took my focus off Iran, as pressing as our mission was. On Friday, August 11, 2017, a group of white supremacists gathered in Charlottesville, Virginia, for a rally the next day. That night, they announced their presence with a march through Charlottesville. They carried tiki torches. They shouted slogans like "White lives matter!" and "Jews will not replace us!" Pictures of the march were broadcast throughout the world. It was unbelievably chilling to see men marching with torches and chanting racist and anti-Semitic slogans in the United States of America in 2017.

The next day, they gathered again, this time in Charlottesville's Emancipation Park, around a statue of Confederate general Robert E. Lee. Hundreds came, some carrying clubs and shields, and faced off with counterprotestors. They yelled obscenities and insults at each other, and the gathering predictably became violent. Later, I read reports that some of the white supremacists had screamed the Charleston killer's name and called him a "hero."

After a few hours the police ordered the crowds to disperse, and it looked for a moment like a disaster would be avoided. But as the crowd at Emancipation Park was breaking up, a few blocks away, one of the demonstrators drove his car into a crowd of pedestrians. Then he reversed and drove into another crowd of people. Heather Heyer, of Charlottesville, was killed. Thirty-five others were injured that day. Two Virginia state troopers monitoring the rally were also killed when their helicopter crashed.

Hours after the rally, President Trump condemned the "egregious display of hatred, bigotry, and violence on many sides, on many sides." Two days later, the president updated his remarks by announcing that a civil rights investigation had been opened by the Department of Justice.

"Racism is evil, and those who cause violence in its name are criminals and thugs, including the KKK, neo-Nazis, white supremacists and other hate groups," he said, reading a prepared statement.

If the president had left it there, his amended response would have been fitting. He had called out the haters and made it clear that they would not be tolerated. But he didn't leave it there. In response to questions from reporters at a news conference the next day, the president equivocated. The moral clarity he had expressed the day before was gone.

"I think there's blame on both sides," President Trump said. "You had some very bad people in that group, but you also had people that were very fine people, on both sides."

The president said that neo-Nazis and white nationalists "should be condemned totally." But he ended his remarks with another pivot to moral equivalence:

"There are two sides to a story. I thought what took place was a horrible moment for our country. A horrible moment. But there are two sides to the country," he said.

As I watched the president's remarks, I was deeply disturbed. I was certain he didn't understand how damaging his remarks were. But I had been through this. A leader's words matter in these situations. And the president's words had been hurtful and dangerous.

I picked up the phone and called the president. I told him how much Charlottesville reminded me of Charleston, not in the magnitude of the human loss, but in the potential for more violence and more hate. He told me that I had handled the tragedy in Charleston beautifully. What he was experiencing, he said, was not the same thing.

I replied to the president that the two situations were not really different. They were the same because the pain was the same. There couldn't be any equivocating about that pain. The Charlottesville marchers' intention was to create division and hate, just like the Charleston killer. The response to these attempts at division had to be crystal clear. Moral clarity was essential, and the president's words were not providing that. You have to stop acknowledging the haters, I told the president. You have to understand the power of your voice.

I don't know if our conversation moved President Trump. We never spoke of the incident again. I do know the president handled the subsequent synagogue shootings in Pittsburgh and near San Diego with great sensitivity and appropriateness. But regardless of whether our conversation affected the president, Charlottesville certainly stayed with me, as it did with so many Americans.

I have known the pain of discrimination. Still, I love America. There isn't another country in the world where the daughter of Indian immigrants could grow up to represent her country at the United Nations. That opportunity has taken me to places of the world where my parents' ethnicity would have predetermined my life, places where tribal conflict is all there is. Who lives and who dies—who is raped and who is not—is determined in these places by the accident of your birth. There is no freedom, no equality. Just division and hatred.

Immediately after the Charlottesville incident, I wrote an email to all USUN employees. It was as much for me as it was for them. The sense of the fragility of life and community that overcame me after Charleston—when nine people were murdered *worshipping in a church*—has never left me.

South Carolina has come so far in leaving its racial history behind. America has, as well. But what we have is still fragile. Not because America is inherently racist. It is absolutely not. But because our values can't be taken for granted. They won't teach themselves to new generations of Americans. If we don't defend them, if we don't cherish them and recognize them as the source of our progress, we will lose them.

"Those who march spewing hate are few, but loud," I wrote. "We must denounce them at every turn, and make them feel like they are on an island and isolate them the same way they wish to isolate others.

"While we should respect diversity of viewpoints, it is incumbent on us to challenge hate with the values we cherish."

America is living through a time when our politics, media, and popular culture are exaggerating our differences, and weaponizing them. People talk about diversity more than ever, but too many of us are becoming intolerant in the name of tolerance. Instead of trying to understand those who disagree with us, we tend to write them off as not even fit to have a conversation with. Instead of focusing on the things that bring us together, too many Americans obsess about the things that separate us.

We have to resist the forces that are pulling us apart, whether they are coming from the left or the right. Because it is our values— our belief that life, liberty, and the pursuit of happiness come to us from God, not government—that tie us together as Americans. It is in countries where these values are *absent* that tribalism and hatred flourish. We can never fail to make this case.

10

"I Don't Get Confused"

Early in 2018, a "journalist" looking to cash in on dirt about the Trump administration published a book. While hawking it on a cable talk show, the author said he was "absolutely sure" President Trump was having an affair—just not sure enough to actually put it in writing. But he dropped a hint designed to help him sell more of his trashy book: If only the TV viewers would read his book (hint, hint: buy it), when they came to the right paragraph, they would know.

Needless to say, this set off a feeding frenzy in Washington. Almost instantly, a passage was found in the book that said I had been spending a lot of time on *Air Force One* alone with the president. "Bingo!" said the Washington rumor mill.

It wasn't true. I had been on *Air Force One* precisely one time at that point, together with several other people. And I had never been alone with the president. The truth is, nobody really believed the rumor; Mika Brzezinski threw the author off the set of *Morning Joe* for repeating the story. But what was so depressing about the whole episode was how familiar the lie was. I dealt with these kinds of made-up, women-bashing rumors when I was a legislator and when I was governor. It was all too familiar.

At every point in my life I've noticed that if you speak your mind and you're strong about it, a small percentage of people will resent you. And the way they deal with their resentment is to throw charges at you—lies or not—to see what sticks. They do this to diminish you. Women, especially, have been dealing with this for a long time. White House communications director Hope Hicks was also a target of the author's lies. It's not just a problem in politics. It's in entertainment, media, and the corporate world. Anywhere women are achieving.

I get asked all the time, especially by young women, what it was like to be one of the few women in the good ol' boy South Carolina legislature, or the first woman governor of South Carolina, or the only woman on the United Nations Security Council (until I was joined by my friends UK ambassador Karen Pierce and Polish ambassador Joanna Wronecka).

The truth goes back to the Wee Miss Bamberg pageant when I was five years old. When you're in a pageant that is based on selecting a white queen and a black queen, and you're disqualified because you don't fit either category, you learn early that labels matter. But I was lucky because my parents taught me that no matter how much people try to label you—and they will—you don't have to live by those labels.

I've always thought being a woman made me special. I am proud of being a woman, but it doesn't define me. I am a big fan of all women, whether in business, science, politics, or elsewhere. I love seeing them do well in every field. It inspires me. Women have challenges, but so do men. And I believe God has given us gifts to overcome these challenges. We have to manage more roles—mom, wife, daughter, professional person. But we are also great at balancing our lives and establishing priorities.

Labeling people based on race, gender, and other characteristics has gotten way out of hand in America today. It's destructive and, ironically, it's limiting. We are all much more than the sum of our labels.

I am much more than a woman or an Indian American or a first-generation immigrant or a military spouse or a politician or a conservative or a mom, wife, and daughter. I'm proud of every one of these things, and I refuse to be classified as just one. All the things that made me different made me who I am today. Sometimes these things have been used against me, sometimes they worked for me. But at the end of the day they gave me multiple ways to be the best person I could be.

Much more than who we are is what we do. The truth is, to do what you want to do, whether it's to succeed in business or politics or to help people, you have to push through the fear. This is one of the great lessons I have learned in my life. Women are good at just about everything we do. We just need to take a chance and not be afraid of what is new and intimidating. When I embrace a new challenge instead of avoiding it, I am always amazed at how much stronger and confident I become.

I've been blessed to live a life free of "what ifs," because I've followed this rule. Everyone thought I was crazy to challenge a thirty-year incumbent for a seat in the South Carolina legislature. I did it anyway. I went against the powerful speaker of the house to require votes on the record in the legislature. He fought me, but I pushed through and got it done. And when the incumbent Republican governor, Mark Sanford, blew up his career by lying about hiking on the Appalachian Trail while he was visiting his mistress, everyone said I should drop my race for governor. I was too close to Sanford, they said. But I stayed in and I won.

When a challenge presents itself, instead of stepping backward, I jump. When I feel the fear in my gut, I push through it. And when you do what you fear most and you succeed, something amazing happens. Your confidence, your strength, and your abilities grow beyond what you ever thought possible. You can justifiably feel proud of yourself. Most important, you are able to tell those coming up behind you that they can jump, too.

Pushing through your fear and being successful has a downside though, especially for women. You can expect to be labeled with the "A" word: "ambitious." When it's said about a man, it means he's entrepreneurial, he's a "striver." But when a woman is called ambitious, it's an indictment, like she's stepping out of her lane. When women ask me what we can do about getting labeled as ambitious, I say the best thing to do is not to worry about it. People are going to say what they are going to say. It used to bother me when people called me ambitious. But if being ambitious is being good at your job, then fine, you can call me ambitious. I will just consider myself a badass.

ALMOST A YEAR TO THE day after he struck Khan Sheikhoun with chemical weapons, the Syrian dictator Assad rained poison down on the people of Douma, a suburb of Damascus.

The Syrians and the Russians had been bombing Douma with

conventional weapons for weeks. But on the evening of April 7, 2018, the basements that the people of Douma had used to protect themselves from conventional bombs became their tombs. The gas that was dropped quickly settled in low-lying areas—like basements—and literally suffocated the men, women, and children there.

This time, when the UN Security Council met, I didn't bother holding up the pictures of the dead. I could have. I could have showed the council pictures of first responders walking through room after room of families lying motionless, with babies still in the arms of their mothers and fathers.

"I could hold up pictures of all this killing and suffering for the Council to see, but what would be the point?" I said during an emergency session. "The monster who was responsible for these attacks has no conscience, not even to be shocked by pictures of dead children."

"The Russian regime, whose hands are all covered in the blood of Syrian children, cannot be ashamed by pictures of its victims," I said. "We've tried that before."

Once again, the Syrians and Russians denied the attack. Russia claimed that evidence of a chemical-weapons attack had been planted in Douma by the United States and Great Britain. The images of the dead were fake, they said. The victims were actors. The depth of the Russian lies would almost be comical if the setting wasn't so deadly serious and sad.

This time, the United States acted along with France and Great Britain to strike back at Assad. In the early morning hours of April 13, British, French, and American warplanes and naval destroyers targeted the heart of the Syrian regime's illegal chemical-weapons program. The strike was twice the size of the 2017 strike.

It obliterated Syria's major research facility for the design and construction of weapons of mass murder.

The strike was a success. I spoke with the president and told the Security Council what he had said: If Syria used chemical weapons again, "the United States is locked and loaded."

But our concern in 2018 was greater than in 2017. This was not an isolated incident. The international prohibition on using chemical weapons was breaking down, with Russia leading the way.

Just a few weeks before the Douma attack, on March 4, Sergei Skripal and his daughter, Yulia, were found unconscious and foaming at the mouth on a park bench in Salisbury, England. Skripal was a former Russian spy. He and his daughter had been poisoned by Novichok, a chemical weapon developed by scientists in the Soviet Union. They barely survived. Two Russian men were later charged with attempting to kill the Skripals by putting Novichok on the front door of Sergei's house in Salisbury. This was attempted murder by Russia on foreign soil, which is unthinkable for a country to do. Three months later, two other Britons were poisoned with Novichok when they apparently found and handled the perfume container in which the nerve agent had been transported to Salisbury. One of them, a woman named Dawn Sturgess, died.

Our British friends were rightly outraged by the Skripal incident. This was a chemical-weapons attack on their own soil. It had exposed hundreds of their citizens to potentially lethal poisoning. In response, we joined together with Great Britain and other European allies to expel Russian intelligence operatives from the United States.

When the Russians were caught being complicit in another chemical-weapons attack in Douma just four weeks later, the Trump administration debated what more we could do beyond military strikes on Syrian facilities.

WHENEVER THE WHITE HOUSE CALLED and asked me to appear on a Sunday-morning news show, I did. In fact, I only went on the Sunday-morning news programs in response to a White House request. On Sunday, April 15, in the aftermath of the allied strikes against Assad's chemical-weapons program, the White House asked me to appear on CBS's *Face the Nation*.

The interview went fine. I described the effectiveness of the U.S., French, and British strikes on Syrian facilities. I went on at some length about how Russia was supporting and protecting Assad even as he was poisoning his own people. The program's host, Margaret Brennan, asked me if there would be consequences for Russia for shielding Assad.

New Russia sanctions had been the subject of multiple conversations and meetings of the administration's national security officials in the days since the Douma attack. The decision was made to impose new sanctions on Russia. It had been determined during a National Security Council meeting a few days prior to my appearance on *Face the Nation* and again in the Oval Office with the president and other officials.

So I answered Margaret's question with what I knew to be the truth.

"You will see that Russian sanctions will be coming down," I said. "Secretary Mnuchin will be announcing those on Monday, if he hasn't already, and they will go directly to any sort of [Russian] companies that were dealing with equipment related to Assad and chemical weapons use."

That evening, I got a call from Treasury Secretary Steven Mnuchin.

"This is not your fault," he said. "But the president decided on Saturday that he didn't want to do the sanctions at this time."

The president had every right to change his mind. But no one had communicated that to me before I went on *Face the Nation*. Steve said he had worked with White House spokesperson Sarah Sanders on a statement that would clarify the situation, taking into account that sanctions had been approved and this was a last-minute decision by the president. Steve was a great friend to me in the administration. He was a straight shooter and was respected by everyone who worked with him. I said that was no problem.

But the message from the White House the next day did not clarify the situation. It portrayed me as the one who got it wrong. In fact, no one had gotten anything wrong, including the president. He simply changed his mind.

Sarah Sanders made a statement that additional Russia sanctions were "being considered" and a decision would be made "in the near future." Anonymous sources went further. They told the press that I had "gotten out ahead" of the decision and that the administration had no plans to announce new sanctions that week.

But the decision had, in fact, been made. The Republican National Committee even put out talking points on Saturday that announced, "We . . . intend to impose specific additional sanctions against Russia to respond to Moscow's ongoing support for the Assad regime."

I had nothing but respect for the president's prerogative to have the last word on this. I was just frustrated with what was being communicated. I thought it would be much more effective for the White House to put out a statement along the lines of, "As the president is going through the process of dealing with Syria and its allies, part of that is dealing with Russia. He is holding off on the sanctions for now." As it was, the contradictory statements were keeping the story alive in the media.

On Monday, I called White House Chief of Staff John Kelly. I've been in politics long enough to know that if you don't firmly tamp down this kind of media firestorm, it will consume you. I told Kelly I was being patient and giving the White House the chance to correct the record.

"I will respectfully give y'all the time to fix this because I think that is in the best interests of everyone," I told Kelly. "But if it's not done by the end of the day on Tuesday, I will handle it myself." I made it very clear that it was not a big deal for the president to change his mind, but not being honest about it would only make matters worse. I had the same conversation with National Security Advisor John Bolton and Secretary of State–Designate Mike Pompeo.

On Tuesday afternoon, at a press conference in Florida following the president's talks with Japanese prime minister Shinzō Abe, White House economic advisor Larry Kudlow threw me under the bus.

Asked by a reporter if there was confusion in the White House over Russia sanctions, Larry gave the White House line that "additional sanctions are under consideration but have not been determined." As for me, I "got out ahead of the curve," Larry said.

"There might have been some momentary confusion about that," he said.

I was done. Clearly no one had any intention of issuing a statement that reflected the reality of the situation. I don't know what was in Larry's heart when he said what he said. I choose to give him the benefit of the doubt. But I was also pretty sure that no one went to the trouble of preparing a statement defending me. It was completely predictable that when Larry spoke to the press he was going to get a question about the sanctions.

I tried calling Larry, but I was, again, getting the silent treatment. At that point, I knew I had to respond. Some members of my staff didn't want me to make an issue of it. But if there is one thing I know, it's that if you don't stand up when your name and your integrity are on the line, no one else will.

By then it was 4:45 in the afternoon. I called Fox News's Dana Perino. I knew she would be going on *The Five* in a few minutes. I trust and respect Dana. I knew she would handle what I was about to tell her with candor and professionalism.

I told Dana I wanted to go on record with a response to what Larry had said. She said okay, shoot.

I told her my comment was simple: "With all due respect, I don't get confused."

There was silence on her end of the line. I told Dana I would send the comment to her in a text as well.

"Anything else?" she said.

"No, that's it."

Dana used the quote for her "One More Thing" segment at the end of the show. Within fifteen minutes of it airing, Larry called me.

"Nikki, I'm calling you with my tail between my legs," he said. "I'm so sorry. You know how much I love you."

"Larry, I'm not even sure you know the facts of the situation. In any case, in what world is it ever okay to say someone is confused?" I said. "Let me rephrase that. In what world do you think it is okay to say *I* am confused?"

Larry said he was sorry again. He promised to make it up to me.

I told him if he wanted to do that he would tell the media what he just told me—that he didn't know all the facts, and I clearly wasn't confused.

"I can't do that," he said.

"Larry, you can and you will," I said.

To his credit, within ten minutes, Larry called *The New York Times*. "She was certainly not confused," he told the newspaper. "I was wrong to say that—totally wrong."

My reaction to Larry's comments wasn't about score settling. It was about protecting my integrity. There have never been any lines to the ladies' room in any of the jobs I've had. But that never mattered. What I cared about was making sure that if I broke a barrier, no one else would have to do it again. Women are cautious about politics, for good reason. It's not a pretty business. It's often hateful. It would be wonderful if we could change our politics in America to make it less nasty and less personal. But until that happens, especially if you're a woman, you have to stand up for yourself. Always. You don't have to be ugly about it. You should do it with grit and grace.

A few weeks after all this happened, T-shirts and stickers started appearing online with the words WITH ALL DUE RESPECT, I DON'T GET CONFUSED emblazoned on them. It was an amazing thing to see. Young women are looking for role models who are strong but respectful, women who are confident enough in themselves that they don't have to get down in the dirt with their worst critics. They want to see a woman stand up for herself and stay standing. It doesn't even matter who said these words. It matters that they struck a chord with women who are natural leaders and want to know that they can make a difference in the world and not lose their humanity.

I have to admit I was taken aback by the way this phrase caught on with women everywhere. This was a personal fight I had to resolve. The fact that my words are now being sold on merchandise online says more about women than it does about me.

We are strong. We are careful about the work we do.

And no, we don't get confused.

ON VALENTINE'S DAY 2018, THE Russian ambassador asked me to lunch. By this time, there had been three Russian representatives on the UN Security Council. The first, Vitaly Churkin, died just weeks after I arrived. Then there was an interim ambassador. He was very reserved and got red in the face when he was angry. I figured out how to get under his skin when we sparred on the council. I would just stare at him and watch his color change.

My third Russian colleague on the Security Council was another veteran diplomat, Vassily Nebenzia. Vassily and I clashed constantly over Syria's chemical attacks and Russia's steadfast refusal to even acknowledge the Assad regime's guilt, much less demand accountability for its actions.

By early 2018, our disagreements with the Russians had become so serious that people were talking about a new "cold war" at the United Nations. I went to Vassily and said, for the sake of good relations in the Security Council, we have got to find at least some areas where we can agree. Apparently he thought that was a good idea, because he asked me to lunch on Valentine's Day.

I liked Vassily but I didn't trust him. He was a smooth operator—he could be charming and funny—but he had some tells. For instance, you could tell how stressed he was by the way he chewed his nicotine gum. We spent two hours at lunch going back and

forth before we finally agreed we could work together on Afghanistan and Africa. It wasn't much, but it was something. The truth
was, we weren't going to be able to see eye-to-eye with the Russians
on much as long as they violated their neighbor's sovereignty and
covered for mass murderers.

In July, on the back end of a NATO meeting in Brussels, President Trump met with Russian president Vladimir Putin in Hel-
sinki, Finland. There were plenty of serious issues on the agenda,
including Ukraine, Syria, and Russian violations of a treaty ban-
ning intermediate-range nuclear missiles. The two leaders spent two
hours meeting alone, with only their interpreters in the room. Afterward, they held an extraordinary joint press conference.

Most of the questions from the American reporters focused on
Russian attempts to interfere with the 2016 election. When a reporter from the Associated Press asked the president whom he believed when it came to Russian interference in the election—U.S.
intelligence agencies or the Russians—President Trump answered:

"My people came to me—[Director of National Intelligence]
Dan Coats came to me and some others—they said they think it's
Russia," he said. "I have President Putin; he just said it's not Russia.
I will say this: I don't see any reason why it would be."

As soon as I could, I requested a meeting with the president.
Chief of Staff Kelly stalled on it and would never call me back. Finally, I called the president and told him I had been requesting a
meeting for days and wasn't getting a response. Within an hour I
had the meeting. Kelly didn't appreciate it and let me know.

I told the president what he had said in the press conference
with Putin made me very uncomfortable. The Russians aren't our
friends. They will never be our friends. And you made it sound like
we were beholden to them, I said.

The president was surprised. No one around him had characterized the press conference in that way. But I was always honest with the president, even when others around him weren't. And the truth was that the Russians did meddle in our elections. They were continuing to try to manipulate us. They sought strength through creating chaos in the world. We couldn't let our guard down, not for a second.

To his credit, the president soon issued additional remarks, saying he had misspoken and that he accepted U.S. intelligence agencies' findings about Russian meddling in the election. I was glad he made that clarification, and I understood what he had been trying to do. He was trying to keep communication open with Putin, just as he had with Kim Jong Un and Chinese president Xi Jinping. He liked to deal directly with his negotiating partners. I had seen him work people face-to-face. He had a remarkable ability to disarm them.

Later, I was asked by a reporter about rumors of the president's unwillingness to put up with advisors who give him bad news. That was not my experience, I said. It was never my experience.

"Regardless of whether I say something he likes or not, he's respectful; he listens to it and we have a conversation about it," I said. "And that's what everyone should want in their president— someone who is willing to hear the bad news."

NEEDLESS TO SAY, THE TRASHY book story had legs. I love music. Music has always made life better for me. It de-stresses me. It gives me peace. Anything from Joan Jett to Drake to Adele to Pink and so many others. Music does my heart good. That's why I was so disappointed with the Grammy Awards in late January 2018. They ruined good music by mixing it with trash.

In a prerecorded skit, celebrities read portions of the book about the Trump administration that had spread rumors about me. John Legend, Snoop Dogg, Cher, and Cardi B all appeared, reading the book. At the end of the skit, the person reading the final passage slowly lowered the book from her face to reveal herself as Hillary Clinton.

I suppose they thought it was "edgy." The audience certainly did. But I couldn't help but imagine if the reaction would be the same if it had been a liberal woman the author had defamed in his trashy book. If it had been a liberal woman, I suspect the skit would never have been written to begin with.

It was the height of the #MeToo movement. Powerful men in politics, of both parties, were being brought down by accusations of sexual harassment and misconduct toward women. So were major figures in the corporate and entertainment worlds. Now the most prominent people in the music industry were promoting a book that had spread salacious rumors about me, and the most prominent Democratic woman in America was joining them. Where were the feminists?

I thought about my daughter and the other young women who were watching this unbelievable display of hypocrisy. We have to raise our girls to be strong. They need confidence and they need thick skin. They need to be taught how to stand up for themselves, regardless of who they are or what their politics are.

I was thinking about our girls a month earlier when I told the host of CBS's *Face the Nation* that the women who had come forward to accuse President Trump of sexual misconduct had the right to be heard.

"They should be heard, and they should be dealt with," I told

John Dickerson. "I think any woman who has felt violated or felt mistreated in any way, they have every right to speak up."

Dickerson asked me if the fact that we knew about some of the accusations against the president before the election meant that those charges were settled.

"That's for the people to decide," I said. "I know that he was elected. But, you know, women should always feel comfortable coming forward. And we should all be willing to listen to them."

The president has denied the accusations, as have many of the other accused men. It is important that the #MeToo movement remain in the proper context. Everyone deserves the presumption of innocence and due process of the law. But I believed then and I believe now that what was happening was good for the country and good for women as long as both sides were heard and treated fairly.

There is someone else I think about when I talk to young women about finding the power of their voices. Her name is Raj Randhawa. She was born in Punjab in the shadow of the Golden Temple, the holiest site in the Sikh religion. At a time and a place when girls were rarely educated beyond high school, she finished law school. She was one of the first women to be picked to sit on the judicial bench in India, but she couldn't take it because her family didn't approve. She is one of the strongest women I have ever known. And she is my mother.

My mom gave up a lot to come to America so I could have the opportunities she couldn't have. She went on to open a business in her new home in South Carolina. When I was just twelve years old, my mother marched me in to see the woman who had kept the books for her business. The woman was about to leave, and there was no bookkeeper to take her place.

My mom pointed at me and said, "If you teach her, she can do it." The bookkeeper thought she was crazy. I thought she was crazy. But she was right.

Girls and women can do anything if we let them and if we teach them. And they can *be* anything if they are respected. And if they are heard.

11

Facing Down a Dictator

Whenever I traveled to areas of conflict as U.S. ambassador, I sought out women to talk to. In many ways, it is women who pay the greatest price for conflict. I found that if I wanted to get the honest, unfiltered sense of conditions on the ground, I had to ask local women. Under the right conditions, women are more open with their opinions than men. In refugee camps, their views were the most trustworthy. Their eyes were on the future, not the past. They cared about building better lives for their children, and that meant they cared about achieving peace.

I was visiting Syrian refugees in camps in Jordan and Turkey when I first got the idea to hold conversations exclusively with women. I was at the camps to see the Syrian refugee crisis from the ground level. But everywhere I went, I was surrounded by my own security, embassy staff, local politicians, and lots of men with guns. It was impossible to have an open, honest conversation, especially with traumatized women. So we found a room, kicked out all the men—even the male members of my staff—and had a candid conversation with a group of women.

What I heard was a point of view that was entirely missing from the heated debate over how to handle Syrian refugees. Even in the midst of all the pain and suffering, there was dignity. The women wanted their children to be educated. They wanted to be productive and self-sufficient. Above all, they wanted to go home. Europe was in crisis over the influx of refugees. The Trump administration was engulfed in controversy over whether and how to admit refugees to the United States. But what these women wanted most for their families was *not* to be refugees; they most wanted to be able to go home and live normal lives.

I THOUGHT THE SYRIAN REFUGEE camps were depressing, but they would turn out to be luxury accommodations compared to what I saw a few months later in the camps that house refugees from the violence in Africa.

All wars are tragedies, but the conflict that has been raging for six years in South Sudan is a unique case of shattered dreams and unrealized potential. South Sudan is the youngest country in the world. There was optimism and celebration when it became independent in 2011. The United States had played a major role in the creation of the new nation. But soon after, conflict erupted. For three-fourths of its young life, South Sudan has been engulfed in a bloody civil war. No one born in independent South Sudan has any memory of their country at peace.

Like so many conflicts in Africa and elsewhere, the forces pitting the people of South Sudan against each other are tribal. Both sides have committed atrocities. But the government of South Sudan is primarily responsible for the suffering of its people. The country's first and only president, Salva Kiir, commands a military that has committed ethnic cleansing, mass rapes, and the deliberate starvation of civilians.

By the fall of 2017, two million South Sudanese had been displaced by the war. Two million more were refugees who had fled the country. Six million were facing famine conditions. Countless were dead. The government of Salva Kiir was using humanitarian aid—life-saving food and medical supplies—as a weapon of war. It was refusing to let humanitarian workers and their supplies into areas that were controlled by rebel factions. Soldiers stole food aid from warehouses. They demanded bribes from aid trucks to pass through checkpoints. The government charged thousands of dollars for permits to allow aid planes to take off or trucks to enter cities.

American taxpayers had made a tremendous investment in South Sudan. In addition to supporting its independence, the United States was the country's largest humanitarian-aid provider. We gave South Sudan $730 million in 2017. But the aid wasn't getting to the people. Even worse, our aid was being used by the government to prolong the war.

I believed then and I still believe that we have to keep our eyes on Africa. It is a place with the potential for great opportunity but also the potential for corruption, terrorism, disease, and famine. So I decided to go there. Africa is the site of over half of UN peace-keeping missions. Plus, I wanted to deliver a message to Salva Kiir: The people of the United States are generous, but we're not stupid. We weren't going to support his war with our aid. Something had to change.

Before I went to see Kiir, I wanted to get an on-the-ground understanding of the conflict he was waging. South Sudan is the site of one of the United Nations' largest and most expensive peacekeeping missions. But the South Sudan peacekeeping force had a bad track record. Peacekeepers had abandoned their posts rather than protect civilians. A year before we arrived, peacekeeping commanders had ignored calls and texts from international aid workers under siege by government soldiers. The aid workers were being held at a hotel less than a mile away. Five of them were gang-raped, and a local journalist was killed.

Our first stop in Africa was a refugee camp in Ethiopia that borders South Sudan. Hundreds of thousands of South Sudanese refugees had gone there to escape the conflict. Entire families were living with nothing but a tarp over their heads. Women were giving birth on dirt floors, floors that turned to mud when the rainy season came. I met a family of seven living under an eight-by-ten-foot tarp. The mother of the children couldn't have been more than fifteen or sixteen. Her husband looked like he was at least fifty.

Rape is a constant, heartbreaking reality of the conflict sites I visited in Africa. The women in the Ethiopia refugee camp wore bright colors that did nothing to mask the trauma they had experienced. It hung in the air in the camp, surrounding us. Nearly all the women had been raped, some repeatedly. Their children wandered around, partially clothed or completely naked, with dazed looks in their eyes.

I met with a group of about one hundred women in a stifling hot tent. They were all completely broken by what they'd experienced. One told me about being gang-raped as a young girl. Later, she watched as South Sudanese soldiers ripped her baby out of her arms and threw him into a fire. She said she was forced to eat the flesh of her own child.

As the woman told her horrifying story, a terrible chain reaction began in the room. One by one, in all parts of the room, the other women began to relive their own horror. Soon they were all either crying or exchanging terrified looks that showed they had also experienced the same barbaric violence. The meeting had begun with me sitting in a chair in front of the group. By the end, I was on the ground, desperately trying to comfort sobbing women who had experienced the kind of pain no human being should ever have to experience.

The only thing sadder than the women in the camps were the children. Most of them didn't know how old they were. They were malnourished and bored. In every camp we went to we asked the children if they had one wish, what would it be? In every case, they wished for an education.

There were many former child-soldiers in the camp in Ethiopia. Some were still children. Kiir's campaign against women and children in South Sudan is uniquely evil. First, he uses rape and violence to convince women of their helplessness. Then he separates them from their young boys. Finally, he turns the boys into cold, remorseless killers. An aid worker told us about two South Sudanese boys who were brothers. They watched their mother be tied to a tree and raped. Afterward, the soldiers forced one brother to shoot his mother on her left side. The other brother was forced to shoot her on her right side. They were permitted to stop only when she died, died of the gunshot wounds her own sons had been forced to inflict on her.

Everywhere I went in the refugee camp that day, I took pictures of what I saw. The next day I would meet with President Kiir. I wanted to show him, up close, the results of the war he was waging. Kiir is an ex–rebel leader who had walled himself off from the people of South Sudan in a heavily fortified compound. From what I understood, he rarely left the compound. So I made sure I had pictures of the people I met in the refugee camps, particularly the children. I didn't want Kiir to be able to deny what he was doing to his country.

We flew into Juba, South Sudan's capital, by military aircraft. Juba is an extremely poor and dangerous place. Our security was provided by ex–special forces. After we landed, we traveled to the presidential compound by armored vehicle. We had to pass through guarded gates and multiple layers of security to get to Kiir. Inside the presidential compound there were lots of large men carrying big guns.

Kiir had historically been pro-American, but he had recently developed a reputation for treating visiting Americans with unconcealed disrespect. A week before my trip he had given an interview to *The Washington Post* in which he was cocky and sure of himself. He dismissed U.S. criticism of him, including from me, as a "conspiracy" against his government, the product of a disinformation campaign by his opponents. As for the refugees, he said, they were not the problem they were being made out to be. They had only left the country because, he said, they were "told [to] by the social media."

The staff at the U.S. embassy in Juba told me to expect more of the same from Kiir in our meeting. He was completely unpredictable and would often be drunk, they said. He might not listen to you. He was known to watch cable news throughout meetings.

I braced myself for the worst. But from the moment we walked into his office, it was clear that a different Salva Kiir was waiting to meet us. Maybe he knew of my reputation for directness. Maybe he'd heard me declare in the Security Council before I left that this was his last chance. Maybe he understood that under President Trump, the United States wasn't fooling around anymore when it came to foreign assistance. Whatever the reason, Kiir very clearly was ready for a serious conversation.

As he always did, Kiir wore his trademark black cowboy hat, which had been a gift from President George W. Bush. He had great affection for President Bush, because he knew the former president had been instrumental in helping South Sudan gain its independence.

Kiir brought in his cabinet members to meet me, including one who was a former member of the opposition. It was clearly an effort to show how seriously he took the need to at least *appear* to support reconciliation in South Sudan. He read a prepared statement that hit all the right notes. He welcomed us and said our meeting was part of the long partnership between South Sudan and the United States. He was respectful and deferential.

After a few minutes, as planned, we dismissed our staff, and it was just me and Kiir in the room. I began by telling him exactly why I was there. I reminded him that the United States was instrumental in the creation of his country. I reminded him that we have been South Sudan's largest donor, having invested well over $11 billion in his country and him. We thought we were helping to create a free and fair country where children and families were safe.

"The way South Sudan is today is not what we paid for," I told Kiir. "It's certainly not the return on the investment we expected from your government."

I told him about how I had gone out and met his people. I listed the refugee camps I had visited. Then I laid all the pictures I had taken out in front of him.

"Look at these children," I said. "You don't know them, but they know you. You are the only leader they know. What you do matters to them. And you are not leading them right now."

"They are just like you used to be," I continued. "They have hopes and dreams. Their mothers want a better life for them."

Kiir began to show some emotion. His eyes welled up with tears. But I pressed on.

"What would you say to these children? I know for a fact that you have said nothing to them, because you've never once left this palace to see the suffering of your own people."

Kiir was once the leader in which the United States and other countries trusted with the future of South Sudan. He had devoted much of his life to fighting for independence for his country. President George W. Bush hosted him at the White House. And Kiir had known personal suffering. Two of his sister's children had died in the famine caused by the war between southern and northern Sudan that preceded independence. His sister later committed suicide.

But Kiir had grown complacent. He expected our assistance to keep coming, despite the atrocities committed by his government. He didn't deny that horrific things had occurred, but he blamed others in his government. I told him that didn't wash. He was the leader of his country, and he'd been getting a pass for a long time. That wasn't going to continue, I said. He had to allow access to food and medical supplies for all his people. And the fighting had to stop.

"If you tell me how to help you, I will," I said. "But this is the last time I'm coming here. We're done."

Then I told Kiir a story. I had been at an event in New York recently and had seen President Bush. I told President Bush I was going to South Sudan. He responded that he'd once had faith in Kiir and hope for the future of the new country. But the way things had turned out was a great disappointment to him.

After I spoke, Kiir was silent for a few seconds.

"Of all the things you've told me, what the president said really hurts," he said. "That really hurts."

We talked for over an hour. I was hard on President Kiir. The United States is both generous and patient, I told him, but we are not without our limits. Entire generations were being lost in South Sudan. Families were being destroyed. I told him the United States cannot and will not look away. But he could change the path his country was on; he could still fulfill the hope that had once been placed in him. It was up to him, I said. What happened next was in his hands. Kiir responded with all the right promises. But words are cheap, particularly words from dictators. As I left his office, I paused at the door and said, "Don't make me come back."

WE HAD ONE MORE PIECE of business in Juba. As the fighting continued in South Sudan, something unprecedented happened. By the thousands, civilians sought refuge at the UN peacekeeping bases there. These desperate people were drawn to the relative safety of the peacekeeping missions. They began to camp outside the gates. And when it became apparent that they could not or would not leave, the United Nations began to establish what are called "protection of civilians" sites.

Very much like the refugee camps, these sites are huge tent cities where hundreds of thousands of South Sudanese huddle in misery, under the often unreliable protection of UN peacekeeping troops. It is a depressing measure of the violence that awaits them outside the sites that they choose to stay in these dirty, cramped places. But women who have no choice but to go outside the sites every day to collect firewood for cooking are the frequent targets of attackers and rapists. The suffering is even greater outside than inside. So they stay, refugees in their own country.

The U.S. embassy and the non-governmental organization (NGO) that ran the site in Juba didn't want us to go there. Of all the "protection of civilians" sites in South Sudan, the camp in Juba was the largest. Some thirty thousand civilians lived inside, most of whom had arrived in the first weeks of the war. They were tired of war and exasperated by their conditions. As we piled into our armored vehicles and traveled through the gates and razor wire to enter the camp, everyone was nervous. A representative of a French NGO was blunt. "Can't we get her a baby to f—ing kiss already and get out of here?" he said, referring to me.

The French NGO worker was not only rude, he was wrong. I knew how serious the situation was. And I wasn't there for a photo op. Whenever I visited places like the camp in Juba, I had one audience in mind: the American people. Most Americans are too busy with their lives and their families to know or care much about South Sudan. But I knew if they saw the pictures on the news of the people suffering there, Americans would care. The conflict in South Sudan is complex. But the pain of the people is not. It is open, obvious, and inescapable. If I could let more Americans know about that pain, I was going to do it.

Massive crowds greeted us as we entered the camp. Many were holding signs. This was usually the case. I found that whenever I traveled to a refugee camp, the people inside always knew I was coming. They would prepare signs and demonstrations; it was their chance to have their voices heard. Occasionally these demonstrations were pretty obviously coordinated by outside groups. I had encountered more than one sign written in perfect English being held upside down by a refugee.

But the demonstrations inside the Juba "protection of civilians" site were different, and in a fascinating way. There were many anti-Kiir signs. But there were also pro-American signs. People held up pieces of cardboard that said PRESIDENT TRUMP SAVE US. A couple refugees held a sheet that read SOUTH SUDAN IDPS [internally displaced persons] AND REFUGEES LOVE PRESIDENT TRUMP . . . THE PEACEMAKER. They chanted, "No more Salva Kiir!" and they also chanted, "Welcome USA!" These people were upset with their leadership, but they were also pro-Trump in a way most of the NGOs who run the camps were not. They welcomed us with the hope that President Trump could help achieve for them the future that President Bush had promised and President Obama had failed to deliver.

The longer we stayed in the camp, the larger and louder the crowds got. I knew they weren't dangerous to us. They were expressing their hatred of Salva Kiir. So we stuck to our itinerary. The final stop was supposed to be our usual meeting with women from the camp. The only thing separating us from the crowds at that point were UN police in riot gear and a rickety wooden fence. The refugees continued to get louder and more numerous. They began to press forward. They had a letter for me, they said. It was a petition on the ongoing civil war and the suffering it was causing. I said I would be happy to accept it, but the security detail wouldn't allow it.

Meanwhile, my staff was watching our security guards begin

to eye the scene nervously. There were three dirt pathways out of the camp wide enough for cars to get through. Crowds of marching, chanting people were filling two of them. I was inside a hut to meet with the women, when one of the security guards came in and said, "Ma'am, we have to go." I started to resist. The people in the crowds weren't dangerous, they just wanted to be heard. But he was emphatic. "Ma'am, we *need* to go."

The security detail quickly hustled my assistant and me into our car, and we immediately began to move. I had no idea where the rest of my staff was. There was also a group of reporters traveling with us. But in the chaos it was impossible to know where anyone was or if the staff or reporters were safe. As we were exiting the gates of the camp, everyone's phones began to light up with messages. Someone had leaked to the Associated Press that I was being run out of a "protection of civilians" camp by anti-American protestors. To their credit, the reporters traveling with us pushed back against the story. The refugees in South Sudan weren't anti-American. In fact, they were pro-American. They just were sick of war. They wanted to be heard.

What I saw on the ground in South Sudan, and what I had heard from President Kiir, made me more determined than ever to pass a weapons embargo on the conflict when I returned to the UN. The United States had tried and failed to pass an embargo in the Security Council in 2016. Since then, no one really knew how many weapons had made their way to soldiers in South Sudan. But we did know these weapons were used to shoot fathers in front of their wives and children. They were used to hold up convoys of food aid. They were used to assault women and girls.

The countries who opposed a weapons embargo on South Sudan

claimed it would somehow hurt the peace process. But their reasoning did not hold up. In the year and a half since the embargo was initially rejected, there had been multiple cease-fires declared by the government and the rebels. Some were even labeled "permanent." But none lasted more than a few days. All were broken by the warring parties, some in only a matter of hours. It was hard to see how a weapons embargo could hurt a peace process that barely existed.

For the balance of 2017 and into 2018 we worked to end the flow of weapons into the conflict in South Sudan. That spring, the UN issued a report on a spike in violence in the war, violence that occurred, not surprisingly, four months after yet another cease-fire had been declared. The details of the report were literally stomach-churning. In six weeks, in just one state in South Sudan, forty villages were attacked. Over 230 civilians were killed, including 35 children. Some 120 women and girls were raped or gang-raped; 25 people were hanged. Over 60 children and elderly and disabled people were burned alive. *Burned alive.*

It takes a lot to move the UN Security Council to action. Even after this gruesome report on all the violence that followed yet another meaningless cease-fire, some on the council still argued that a weapons embargo would hurt the "peace process." But we persisted. We introduced a resolution to impose an embargo and sanction people responsible for the violence in South Sudan. The resolution wasn't an obstacle to peace, I argued. It was the essential first step toward peace.

"The goal of this resolution is simple," I told the Security Council. "If we're going to help the people of South Sudan, we need the violence to stop. And to stop the violence, we need to stop the flow of weapons to armed groups."

Every member of the council was more than aware of the atrocities being committed in South Sudan. They had known of these atrocities for years. The Security Council was out of excuses.

"We can do more than just sit here and listen to these horror stories," I said. "We can do more than just express our sympathy with empty words. We can take action."

On July 13, 2018, that rarest of rare things happened: The UN Security Council took concrete action. The U.S. resolution passed and a weapons embargo was placed on South Sudan for the first time.

The vote was close. To gain passage in the Security Council, you need 9 out of 15 votes in favor, and no vetoes. We got the nine we needed, and no more. Six countries abstained, including China and Russia. Either of them could have vetoed the embargo resolution, but they didn't. It was a singular victory at the UN.

Occasionally I will get questions from Americans about why we should care about a poor, violent, distant place like South Sudan. My answer is always twofold.

First, we should care because the children I saw in the camps will be adults one day. If nothing changes, they will be uneducated, untrained, and resentful of the conditions they grew up in. As such, they will be prime targets for recruitment by terrorist and extremist groups. This is in fact happening already. Depravation of this kind has a real tendency to spread. If we don't pay attention to the way these kids are being raised in South Sudan, Congo, Syria, and elsewhere, we will be dealing with them as adults, potentially as terrorists in our own country.

Second, it is impossible to see the suffering of the people there and not be moved to action. It's as simple as that. The stories of the women I met—and the faces of the children I saw—are indelibly printed in my memory. The passage of the South Sudan weapons embargo didn't generate a lot of headlines. It wasn't my most high-profile moment at the United Nations. But none of that matters. It was one of my proudest accomplishments.

THE SAME TRIP THAT TOOK me to South Sudan took me to another war-torn African country, the Democratic Republic of Congo. In the fall of 2017, the Congo's leader, Joseph Kabila, had been in office for a year past the time his country's constitution mandated that he leave. The Congo faced a historic first—a peaceful, democratic transfer of power. But Kabila had ignored constitutionally mandated elections in 2016. And now that an agreement had been reached to hold elections in 2018, Kabila was stalling. Meanwhile, the same sad litany of crimes was being committed against the Congolese people. Civilians mutilated, burned alive, and hacked to death. Women raped. Children abducted to be turned into soldiers. Even UN officials investigating human rights abuses were being killed.

For two years we worked to ensure that not only were elections held in the Congo, but that they were free, fair, and inclusive. Progress was painfully slow. At first, Kabila picked the last possible moment, at the end of December, to hold elections in 2018. He waited until August 2018—four months before elections were supposed to be held—to announce that he wouldn't seek reelection, a move that would have been in blatant violation of the Congolese constitution.

When we were in the Congo we continued to insist that elections be held on schedule. We met with one of the few institutions that still had the trust of the Congolese people—the Catholic

Church. The church ended up being instrumental in bringing about elections.

We met with the commission in charge of putting on the elections. It was staffed with Kabila cronies who continued to insist that the elections be delayed. They claimed logistical problems registering voters, getting voting machines—anything to renege on Kabila's promise of democracy. We had to stay tough and insist that elections be held in 2018. Free and fair voting in the Congo was not a matter of resources or logistics. It was a matter of political will. We never let the Kabila government forget that.

As the scheduled elections grew nearer, Kabila and his cronies invented new reasons that the voting should be delayed. They showed their true colors by attacking the idea of democracy itself. They tried to convince the people of the Congo that elections were too big a risk. The people should continue to accept a government that was violent, corrupt, and unaccountable, they argued.

In one of my last speeches in the Security Council in November 2018, I spoke directly to the people of the Congo. I thought back to all the reasons my mother and father sacrificed so much to come to America. The same freedom and opportunity they sought were owed the people of the Congo as well. Anyone saying otherwise was a dangerous liar.

To the Congolese people, as you prepare to take this momentous leap into your future, my message to you is this: life, liberty, and the pursuit of happiness is your birthright and that of every human being. Claim it. Demand it. Seize it for yourselves and your grandchildren yet to come. Know that there are people throughout the world rooting for your success. And know that the prayers and the best wishes of the American people are with you.

The Congolese foreign minister once told me you have to visit the Congo to really understand it. I told him I had visited the Congo. I had not only met with its leaders, I had listened to its people. Their message was heartfelt and unmistakable. They want a better life. And they want a voice in the leadership that will allow them to build one.

When we were in the capital city of Kinshasa there was a Congolese woman with a history of protesting the Kabila government who wanted to meet with me. She had figured out what hotel I was staying in and was waiting in the lobby to speak to me. Our security didn't want me to do it. The people from the U.S. embassy in Kinshasa didn't want me to meet with her, either. They were worried that it would anger the government. But I thought it was important to do. Meeting people like her was literally one of the reasons I was in the Congo. So we met in the lobby. She was frantic about the need for free and open elections in her country. Later, I ran into a Congolese acquaintance who told me this woman had been arrested and was living in the streets.

Congo went on to have elections in December 2018. They weren't perfect—far from it—but they finally delivered for the people of Congo what they most wanted: an end to the eighteen-year reign of the dictator Kabila. Although a member of an opposition party was declared president, the Congo's future is still uncertain. But the people have been given a taste of democracy. It was a step forward that the Congo would never forget. I was proud of the role we were able to play. Not long after the elections I met a woman from the Congo in the Charlotte, North Carolina, airport. She told me they'd given me a nickname in the Congo: "Momma Nikki." I was so touched. I was proud, but also concerned for the future of these amazing people.

Self-government is one of the fundamental beliefs that ties us together as Americans. But bringing this about in other countries is unquestionably difficult. Americans rightly lose patience with far-flung conflicts that seem to have no end. We grow weary of trying to ease the suffering that the men who lead these countries seem to bring on themselves.

The United States shouldn't go to war to stop every dictator or address every injustice. In fact, we should very rarely go to war, and only when essential American security interests are at stake. But we can act where and when we can on behalf of freedom and human rights. We can act through diplomacy and economic sanctions. Even just using our voices and speaking out is worthwhile to support American principles.

I tried to act in defense of American principles at the United Nations. And that is what I intend to do for the rest of my life. Not just because I believe in freedom and human dignity, but because I have seen what life is like when they are absent. I have seen things that I cannot un-see.

The last stop on our trip to Africa was at a camp for Congolese, mostly women and children, who were driven out of their homes by the war. I visited a mother of seven who cried as she described being raped in front of her children. She said she could no longer look them in the eye because of the shame she felt.

I met women who started their own bakery because it was too dangerous to leave the camp to get bread. I had only been in Africa for three days at that point. But I had seen so much. I could barely hold it together as I met with these women and other displaced people.

When we got into our jeeps to leave the sprawling camp, what must have been almost one hundred children started running alongside us. They were young kids, between three and seven years old. They ran alongside our vehicles all the way to the airfield. When I got into the helicopter, they were still there, waving and screaming. I waved back. I made it until we took off and were out of sight of the children before I broke down.

No children should have to live the way these children live. No children should have to feel that pain. I have never forgotten them, and I never will.

12

The Fight for a Hemisphere
of Freedom

I t was an unusually warm day for late September in New York City. Inside the United Nations, the Venezuelan dictator Nicolás Maduro was at the podium. In front of a global television audience, Maduro railed against U.S. "imperialists." He compared himself to South African civil rights hero Nelson Mandela. He claimed that the humanitarian crisis in his country was a conspiracy between the United States and Venezuela's enemies.

Outside, on the plaza along First Avenue, another gathering was happening. There were no international diplomats. But there was anger. And there was urgency. Hundreds of Venezuelans had gathered to protest the growing humanitarian, economic, and political crisis in their country, the crisis created by Maduro.

It is a sad reflection on the United Nations that a narco-criminal dictator was given a podium to address the world while the people who paid the price for his criminality were relegated to the street outside. But there they were. The day after Maduro spoke to the

General Assembly, the Venezuelan protestors asked me to address their gathering. I had been vocal in the Security Council about what was happening in Venezuela. Still, it was an unusual request. Diplomats at the United Nations don't speak outside on the street. They don't use megaphones. They don't encourage their audience to "get loud!"

It's a good thing I was never much of a diplomat. I agreed to do it.

Six weeks earlier I had stood on the Simón Bolívar International Bridge, which crosses from Venezuela into Colombia. I'd watched as a continuous line of desperate Venezuelans—women, children, whole families—trudged past me toward Colombia. I watched fathers and mothers crossing to sell their possessions to buy food and medicine. I saw professionals, whose salaries had been reduced to nothing by 1 million percent (!) inflation in Venezuela, crossing into Colombia to work in menial jobs. I saw entire families go by, some to get the only meal they would have that day. Others crossed to beg on Colombian streets to feed their families.

As I watched this desperate stream of humanity, I kept coming back to how tragically unnecessary it was. Venezuela was once a wealthy country. It was the richest country in South America when it was both democratic and capitalist. By August of 2018, when I stood on the Simón Bolívar Bridge, Venezuela's government leaders had rejected both democracy and capitalism. The predictable result was millions of Venezuelans were hungry, sick, or dying due to a lack of basic food and medicine. Mothers picked through garbage cans to feed their children, even as Maduro refused to allow humanitarian aid into the country. Between two and three million Venezuelans had simply fled, causing an unprecedented crisis of migration in South America.

Back at the UN, I faced the crowd of protestors and I wondered where to start. So I told them about my trip to the bridge.

"What I saw is what no one should have to live," I said into a megaphone to be heard above the crowd. Venezuelans were literally starving, I said. "All while Maduro is eating in nice restaurants."

The crowd roared. A week earlier, a video had emerged showing Maduro eating a $250 rack of lamb and smoking a cigar in the Istanbul, Turkey, restaurant of a celebrity chef. Meanwhile, the average Venezuelan had lost twenty-four pounds on what they called the "Maduro diet." That's literally a starvation diet.

Two days earlier, in an address to the UN General Assembly, President Trump had announced new sanctions against Maduro's closest cronies. The president encouraged the assembled nations to join the United States in calling for democracy in Venezuela. I told the crowd we wouldn't stop working until there was a free and democratic Venezuela.

"We are going to fight for Venezuela, and we are going to continue doing it until Maduro is gone!" I said. Then I did one of my favorite things: I encouraged all Venezuelans to use the power of their voices.

"I will tell you: I'm going to be loud. President Trump is going to be loud. The United States is going to be loud. And Maduro will hear us because we won't stop talking until we see Maduro go. Keep your voices loud!"

DURING MY FIRST MONTHS AT the United Nations, hundreds of thousands of Venezuelans had taken to the streets to protest the growing Maduro dictatorship. Food and medicine shortages were becoming acute in 2017. Inflation was spiraling out of control.

Maduro responded with mass arrests and killings in the streets. Then, at the end of March, he dissolved the democratically elected legislature. We watched with grave concern as a crisis mounted for the Venezuelan people, one that would not confine itself to Venezuela for long.

What Maduro was doing was not yet headline news. But the United States pushed for the UN Security Council to respond to the growing violence and repression in Venezuela. As usual, Russia and China objected. Both countries are allies and financial backers of the Maduro dictatorship. They argued, as they always do when one of their allies engages in horrible conduct, that the Security Council only deals with peace and security and that what was happening in Venezuela had nothing to do with either. When we were finally able to hold a closed-door meeting in May, I argued that the job of the Security Council is to address conflict, and the only way to avoid conflict is through prevention.

People were starving in Venezuela, not because of any drought or act of God, but because of Nicolás Maduro. His destruction of the economy combined with his violent crackdown on human rights, I predicted, would only bring more Venezuelans to the streets. That would bring more repression. And soon, violence and hunger would begin to drive desperate Venezuelans into neighboring countries. Then, I argued, the "internal" problems of Venezuela would be the region's and the world's problems. And that meant they would be the Security Council's problems.

History had already proven this, time and again. The first sign of conflict is a country that doesn't respect the rights of its people. It never fails. When a government violates human rights, people protest. And when voices get loud, the government faces a choice: either listen to the voices and make changes, or suppress the voices.

Governments that don't respect human rights always choose to suppress dissent. And that's how conflict begins.

The Syrian war began with a massive violation of the rights of the Syrian people. In 2011, Syrian schoolchildren were arrested by the Assad government for writing on a school, "The people want to topple the regime." The parents found out their children were being beaten and tortured in prison. Protests demanding their release were launched. The government cracked down with live fire and additional arrests. The protests grew, sparking more backlash from the government. Before long, there was an all-out war. Other countries stepped in. Half of the Syrian people were killed or forced to flee their homes. A refugee crisis began that threatened the security of the world and changed the face of Europe.

The chaos of the Arab Spring began in a similar fashion, with a simple street vendor in Tunisia who was abused by the corrupt government. Police stole from him and humiliated him while he tried to sell oranges, apples, and dates to feed his family. He eventually set himself on fire in front of the police station. It was an act of desperation that reverberated across North Africa and the Middle East. It sparked protests and brought down governments. All because of one country's refusal to honor the rights and dignity of its citizens.

With a few exceptions on the council, my argument in that closed-door meeting fell on deaf ears. Believe it or not, the Security Council has traditionally not discussed human rights. Its charge, I was told again and again, is "peace and security." Countries in which "only" human rights are being violated have no place on the Security Council's agenda, my colleagues repeatedly told me. Other, lesser United Nations organizations took care of these.

. . .

THE UN ORGANIZATION OFFICIALLY RESPONSIBLE for monitoring and enforcing human rights is, sadly, the United Nations' greatest failure. After World War II, when the UN was being founded, the United States was instrumental in the creation of the UN Commission on Human Rights. In a world that had just witnessed the horror of the Holocaust, the Human Rights Commission (now known as the Human Rights Council) was to be a separate unit of the United Nations, located in Geneva, Switzerland. It would be dedicated exclusively to human rights. Its first chairman was Eleanor Roosevelt, the former American First Lady, who hopefully called it "a place of conscience."

On paper, the Human Rights Council (HRC) was meant to reflect the best of the United Nations—and the best of the American belief in human dignity. When it has held to its mission, the HRC has advanced the cause of human rights. It put a spotlight on crimes committed by Syria's Assad and the Kim dictatorship in North Korea. The problem is, these actions are the exception that proves the rule. By the time I came to the UN, the Human Rights Council had become not a place of conscience, but a place of hypocrisy and corruption.

It is perfectly legitimate to expect an organization devoted to human rights to require its members to respect human rights. Sadly, this is not a criterion for membership in the Human Rights Council. Countries are elected through secret ballot in the UN General Assembly. To the UN's shame, in 2017, the Human Rights Council counted as members some of the world's worst human rights offenders. Cuba, China, Rwanda, and Saudi Arabia all had seats on the HRC. In fact, over half of the members failed to meet basic standards of human rights, according to the pro-democracy group Freedom House.

I was horrified. When the Congo was elected to a seat on the HRC, my alarm only increased. I had seen the horrific human rights abuses of the Kabila government up close; I knew all about the mass graves. How could the Congo, not to mention Cuba and China, uphold standards of human rights for other countries that they routinely violated themselves?

The answer, of course, was they couldn't—and they didn't. The Castro dictatorship in Cuba had long arrested and detained critics and human rights advocates. The Cuban government strictly controls the media. It restricts the people's access to the internet. Thousands of political prisoners sit in Cuban jails. Cuba has never been condemned by the Human Rights Council. And then there was China. How could a country that operates massive "re-education" camps to culturally cleanse itself of an ethnic minority be a member of the world's premier human rights group? It could, and it was. China was sitting on the Human Rights Council even as it began its campaign to eliminate its Uighur minority.

I also believed that countries with which the United States has had friendly relations can't be given a pass when it comes to human rights. We have extensive economic and diplomatic ties with Saudi Arabia. They are an important partner for us against Iran, and can play a constructive role in the broader Middle East. Furthermore, they have taken some concrete steps to expand rights for women in their society. That should be applauded. But we can't allow our good relations to cover up extreme Saudi misdeeds. In 2017, I called out Saudi Arabia among the countries that had no business sitting on what was supposed to be the world's premier human rights organization. That warning came to chilling effect more than a year later with the barbaric murder of Jamal Khashoggi at the hands of the Saudis.

By 2017, the Human Rights Council had become an organization that countries joined not to promote human rights, but to shield themselves from criticism of their own human rights abuses. When Cuba was reelected in 2016, the deputy foreign minister called it "irrefutable evidence of Cuba's historic prestige in the promotion and protection of all human rights for all Cubans." It was beyond disgusting.

Which is not to say that the HRC did nothing. It stayed busy diminishing its credibility even further by singling Israel out for condemnation. Citizens of Israel—including its numerous Arab citizens—have the right to speak freely, worship freely, and live openly as gay or lesbian. In Iran, all of these things are forbidden; some are even punishable by execution. And yet, since its creation, the HRC has condemned Israel ten times more often than it has criticized Iran. The HRC has a standing agenda item devoted only to Israel. No other country is treated the same way. Think about how that happens. So many violent, repressive regimes get a pass from the HRC, and the one democratic, freedom-loving country in the Middle East is singled out in every session. It defies all logic.

In June 2017, I traveled to Geneva to address the Human Rights Council. I talked about the noble beginnings of the council and how far it had fallen from its ideals. I laid out a series of reforms necessary for the HRC to reclaim its legitimacy. I called for changes to its elections to keep human rights abusers off the council. And I called for the removal of the agenda item devoted exclusively to Israel. I was blunt. I had learned by then that I needed to be.

"These changes are the minimum necessary to resuscitate the

council as a respected advocate of universal human rights," I said. "For our part, the United States will not sit quietly while this body, supposedly dedicated to human rights, continues to damage the cause of human rights."

If the reforms weren't enacted, I warned, the United States would "pursue the advancement of human rights elsewhere."

As I spoke in Geneva, conditions were continuing to deteriorate in Venezuela. These were just the latest steps in a human rights crisis that had been building for eighteen years. It began with the election of Hugo Chávez in 1999, and it accelerated under Maduro. For almost two decades, the government had systematically robbed the people of their rights to speak, to protest, and to have due process of the law.

My colleagues in New York had insisted that the Human Rights Council was the right place to address the crisis in Venezuela. It was way past time someone did. The HRC had never once condemned the government of Venezuela. So I requested to speak to the council about the situation there. Maduro had just announced sham elections would be held in July to install a new legislature that he controlled. He was literally destroying the right of Venezuelans to determine their own destiny. But my request to speak was denied, and that said everything about what was wrong with the Human Rights Council. Why? Because Venezuela was a member of the council. Maduro's crimes were off-limits.

I had been shunted off to Geneva by the Security Council. The Human Rights Council refused to have a hearing because Venezuela was a member. So we were forced to hold a panel discussion on Maduro's crimes at a location outside the HRC. But even there, in a private space outside the HRC, the Venezuelan government tried to silence the voices of its critics. An official of the Maduro regime publically berated two Venezuelans we had invited to speak at the event. He screamed at them for sitting on a stage with "the worst country in the world." The Maduro thug warned our speakers that "there will be consequences" for their participation.

Contrast this—not being allowed to speak in the HRC, having speakers harassed and intimidated—to the reception Maduro had received in Geneva two years earlier.

In 2015, the Venezuelan dictator had been invited to speak to a special gathering of the Human Rights Council. In his speech, Maduro continued to refuse to allow HRC investigators into Venezuela. He accused the United States of "misusing human rights as a political weapon." He called for "maximum respect" for his regime from the HRC.

He got a standing ovation.

THE SECURITY COUNCIL HAD SENT us to Geneva, and the Human Rights Council had refused to hear us, but we didn't stop fighting to shine a spotlight on Venezuela in 2017. The reason went beyond Maduro's violations of the human rights of Venezuelans, as concerning as that was. It had to do with the kind of government the Maduro regime represented. And it was not alone. There are two opposing models of government vying for dominance in the Western Hemisphere. The Obama administration's one-sided opening to Cuba had telegraphed indifference about which model was in the best interests of the United States and the hemisphere. I was determined to remove any question about exactly where the United States came down.

Vice President Mike Pence had a term for a vision of the Western Hemisphere that we shared. He called it the "hemisphere of freedom." It was partly aspirational, partly descriptive. There are serious exceptions, but overall the Americas today are more free, democratic, and free-market than they have ever been, and that's a good thing.

On the same trip that took me to the bridge linking Venezuela and Colombia, I represented the administration at the inauguration of Iván Duque, a young, pro-American, pro-business reformer who had just been elected president of Colombia. I was happy to be there. Colombia, along with countries like Brazil, Argentina, Chile, Ecuador, and Peru represent the "freedom model" in Latin America. They respect democracy, the rule of law, and the rights of their people. They still face challenges, but they have embraced the principles essential for prosperity and peace.

There is another model that has long been in conflict with the freedom model in the Western Hemisphere and in the world. It's the model of socialism, dictatorship, corruption, and human rights violations. Under Maduro, Venezuela follows this model. But it is not alone in the Americas. Venezuela is supported by Cuba with thousands of military and security advisors. Cuba, with help from China and Russia, has done more than any other country to prop up the Venezuelan dictatorship. And the Venezuelan regime, in turn, has used its oil to prop up another unfree state in the Americas: Nicaragua.

The conflict between these two models was once a war of ideas. But the intellectual contest between democratic capitalism and socialist dictatorship has been over for a long time. Free minds and free markets won. History has shown where these separate paths lead. The freedom model has lifted more people out of poverty than any other system of government in the history of humankind. Meanwhile, the Cuba-Venezuela-Nicaragua path only leads downward to poverty and oppression. Venezuela is a perfect example. It is a country that is rich in natural resources with a prosperous and democratic past. But socialism has put it on a death spiral of corruption, poverty, and oppression. It is one of the saddest stories of our time.

The truth of these two models of government is not lost on anyone at the United Nations. As a matter of fact, the vast majority of governments speak in nothing but glowing terms about respect for freedom of assembly, freedom of expression, and free access to information.

But when it comes to actually walking the walk and calling out individual governments for violating these rights, UN members too often cast aside these beliefs. This is especially true, unfortunately, when it comes to calling out governments that are hostile to the United States. Too many nations, even many we consider our friends, refuse to hold repressive governments accountable for their actions. They go along with the mob when they should be standing up to the mob.

This tendency is one of the reasons the American people legitimately question our investment in the United Nations. For years, the United States turned a blind eye to this dangerous hypocrisy. I was determined to change that. If I couldn't end the practice of giving America's enemies a free pass to oppress their people, I was determined to at least call it out—loudly.

For example, by the time I became ambassador, a resolution had been introduced in the General Assembly every year for twenty-five years that blames the United States for the poverty and oppression of the Cuban people. Read that again: For twenty-five years a resolution had been introduced that claims the United States is responsible for the way the Cuban regime treats its people. The premise is absurd. No one believes it. But the resolution passes overwhelmingly each year nonetheless.

Only at the United Nations can this happen.

For the first twenty-four years the resolution was introduced, the United States naturally opposed it. Then, in 2016, the Obama administration for the first time *abstained* on the resolution. It reasoned that it was better to accept blame for the Castro regime's mistreatment of the Cuban people than to be on the wrong side of a lopsided vote. The administration feared America would be "isolated" at the UN if it stood up for the freedom and dignity of Cubans. What was unbelievable to me was that the Obama administration conceded that point. It wanted to be liked at the UN so much that it accepted the outrageous premise that American policies—and not the Cuban dictatorship—were robbing the Cuban people of freedom and prosperity.

When the resolution was introduced again in 2017, I couldn't hide my disgust when I spoke to the General Assembly. I announced that, that year, the United States would be opposing the resolution.

"[A]s is their right under our constitution, the American people have spoken," I said. "They have chosen a new president, and he has chosen a new ambassador to the United Nations."

I reminded the General Assembly that the United Nations did not have the power to change U.S. policy toward Cuba. That was the sole prerogative of the president and the United States Congress. In reality, the resolution was nothing more than a yearly opportunity for the UN to bash the United States. But we were no longer going to sit silently while the UN vented its anti-Americanism in the name of concern for the Cuban people. I said:

As long as the Cuban people continue to be deprived of their human rights and fundamental freedoms . . . the United States does not fear isolation in this chamber or anywhere else. Our principles are not up for a vote. They are enshrined in our Constitution. They also happen to be enshrined in the Charter of the United Nations. As long as we are members of the United Nations, we will stand for respect for human rights and fundamental freedoms that the Member States of this body have pledged to protect, even if we have to stand alone.

As expected, we lost the vote 191 to 2. Only Israel joined us in rejecting the resolution. We were definitely "isolated." But our dignity was intact. I never understood the fear that many diplomats had about being isolated. My view was, and is, if your position is right, you should not be ashamed of it. You should be proud to stand alone with it if you must. And I was proud that day on the Cuba vote.

In 2018 when the resolution was introduced again, we decided to use the opportunity to find out if we could shame more countries into opposing it. We noted how, every year, countries expressed support for the rights of the Cuban people, even as they voted to blame the United States and not the Cuban dictatorship, for denying those rights. The year before, the ambassador of the European Union had called on Cuba to "fully grant its citizens internationally recognised civil, political, and economic rights and freedoms." Ambassadors speaking for countries from Africa to the Caribbean had expressed the same desire. But the resolution, as it was written, did nothing to achieve respect for those rights. So we attached a series of amendments that would put the General Assembly on record supporting them.

For twenty-seven years, the General Assembly had approved this resolution and nothing had changed for the Cuban people. "It doesn't help a single Cuban family," I said. "It doesn't feed a single Cuban child. It doesn't free a single Cuban political prisoner."

We could do better.

"[T]he United Nations has the unique ability to send a moral message to the Cuban dictatorship," I continued. "We should use our megaphone to do something that has the potential to actually improve the lives of the Cuban people."

"This year, you will be asked to vote, not just on the American embargo. You will be asked to vote on Cuba's political prisoners. You will be asked to vote on Cuba's lack of freedom of expression. You will be asked to vote on Cuba's oppression of workers."

We held eight separate votes on eight amendments. Collectively, they called on Cuba to "fully grant its citizens internationally recognized civil, political, and economic rights and freedoms, including freedom of assembly, freedom of expression, and free access to information." Only Ukraine and Israel joined us in voting yes on every amendment. The Marshall Islands voted for one amendment. More than sixty-five countries abstained. In the end, the resolution passed, unamended, 189 to 2.

The outcome was expected. We didn't really think countries would suddenly rediscover their principles that afternoon at the United Nations. What did surprise me, however, was the round of applause that greeted the final vote passing the resolution.

I took the floor to speak after the voting was over.

"I'm always taken aback when I hear applause in this chamber in moments like this," I said, "because there are no winners here today. There are only losers.

"The United Nations has lost. It has rejected the opportunity to speak on behalf of human rights," I continued. ". . . Once again, we were reminded why so many people believe that faith in the United Nations is often misplaced. The countries that profess to believe in human rights have lost, too. They have earned a justified measure of doubt that they will act to defend their beliefs."

Most of all, I said, the Cuban people had lost. They had been abandoned yet again by the United Nations. But they would not be abandoned by the United States, at least not on our watch. We hadn't changed the outcome of a symbolic vote in the United Nations. But we had exposed the hypocrisy and corruption at the heart of the vote, and that was something worthwhile.

"While today's votes were not admirable, they were highly illuminating," I concluded. "And that light contributes to the cause of truth, which is the essential basis of freedom and human rights."

ON JUNE 19, 2018, A year after I went to Geneva to address the council, Secretary of State Mike Pompeo and I announced the United States was withdrawing from the Human Rights Council. There were voices in Congress and elsewhere urging President Trump to withdraw as soon as he took office. We could have easily done that. Instead, we spent a year trying to make the council a true force for human rights.

Part of our campaign was public diplomacy to encourage other nations to join us in reform. I mentioned our campaign frequently in speeches, and the president weighed in as well. But most of our effort was behind the scenes. We met with more than 125 countries at the UN. We circulated multiple drafts of resolutions outlining reforms.

Many, if not most, of the countries we talked to, said off the record that the Human Rights Council had become an embarrassment.

Behind the scenes, they admitted that countries like Venezuela and China shouldn't serve in any organization with the words "human rights" in its name. They knew the truth.

But very few were willing to take a stand in public. There were the usual suspects—China and Russia—who turned us down. No surprise there. They and the other authoritarian regimes on the council were perfectly happy with the way things were. The HRC was a useful cover for their own human rights records and the records of their friends.

What was more baffling was the resistance we received from groups and countries that should know better, from those who say they believe in human rights and human dignity.

There are many private, non-governmental organizations that do great work on behalf of human rights around the world. They agreed with us on the need to keep human rights violators off the HRC. So you can imagine our surprise when they came out publically *against* our reforms. Groups like Amnesty International and Human Rights Watch told countries to vote against us. They actually sided with China and Russia on a critical human rights issue. The NGOs thought if they opened up the Human Rights Council to any changes it would result in other amendments that would make the council even more hostile to human rights.

It was extremely disappointing. These groups, who claimed to care about human rights, distrusted the UN so much that necessary reforms couldn't be attempted because it *might make things worse.*

It was also proof that even NGOs play politics. They can give all the excuses they want to. But at the end of the day they opposed an effort to make the Human Rights Council more responsive to the cause to which they were supposedly dedicated. After that, it was impossible for me to take their claims seriously.

Even more disappointing were the supposedly pro–human rights countries that refused to speak up. They were embarrassed by the Human Rights Council. They knew it needed to change. And we gave them opportunity after opportunity. But after months of agreeing with us on the need for reform, they would not take a stand unless it was behind closed doors. They assured us they had convictions, they just lacked the courage to openly fight for them.

Many of our friends urged us to stay on the Human Rights Council for the sake of the institution. The United States, they said, provided the last shred of credibility the council had. But in the end, that is precisely why I felt we had to withdraw.

The right to speak freely and to associate and worship freely, the right to determine your own future and to be treated equally under the law—these are sacred rights. They are ours by virtue of our humanity, not by virtue of the country or tribe we were born into. Americans take these rights seriously, too seriously to allow them to be cheapened, especially by an institution that calls itself the Human Rights Council.

We left the HRC, not because we don't care about human rights for all, but because we do. We were criticized for the move, but I've never been more sure about anything in my life. The United States could not continue to give credibility to an organization that made a mockery of human rights. The United States does more for human rights, both inside and outside of the United Nations, than any other country in the world. It's not even close. And that did not change after we left the HRC.

We continued to argue that human rights deserve a place on the UN agenda even more prominent than the Human Rights Council: They deserve a place on the Security Council itself. We made the case over and over that human rights violations lead to conflicts that threaten the peace and security of regions and of the world.

Our fight wasn't just about process—about where human rights falls in the UN bureaucracy. We took concrete action. We successfully fought back Russian and Chinese efforts to reduce the number of UN peacekeepers devoted to the protection of human rights. We ended the United States' complicity in violating the rights of Iranians. We passed a historic arms embargo and sanctions on South Sudan. We were the loudest voice advocating for the Ukrainian people, whose sovereignty was being violated by the Russian regime.

And in the end, the United States did what the Human Rights Council refused to do: We took the side of the Venezuelan people over the criminal dictatorship of Nicolás Maduro. In the summer of 2017, the United States began to sanction Maduro and his cronies. The Department of the Treasury has put sanctions on Maduro, his wife, and his son for jailing and killing Venezuelan protestors. The United States has also worked to stop Maduro cronies from continuing to steal oil and gold proceeds from the Venezuelan people.

We are far from alone in this. The large majority of countries in Latin America have joined together in protest against the cruelty of the Maduro regime.

We will continue to raise our voices to protect freedom because it is who we are. And I will continue to use my voice, inside and outside of government. Not just because I am a former ambassador. But because I am an American. And America can no more abandon the cause of freedom and human dignity than abandon itself.

The day will come when the people of Venezuela and Cuba join the hemisphere of freedom. That will be a great day for those long-suffering people, and it will be a great day for the United States.

13

Exiting on My Terms

M r. President, it's time."
It was early October 2018. I was in the Oval Office
with President Trump and Jared Kushner.

"Time for what?" the president asked. I couldn't tell if he was joking.

"I'm leaving," I said.

"You can't leave," he countered.

"We talked about it months ago," I reminded the president. Being U.S. ambassador to the United Nations had been the honor and the challenge of a lifetime. But I had told the president the day would come when I felt like it was time for someone else to take on the job. That day would be at the end of the year, I said. I was resigning.

The president asked me if I was sure this was what I wanted to do. He was being kind. I told him I was sure. I had taken the job on the condition that I work directly with him and be free to speak my mind. President Trump had delivered on his side of the bargain.

He had given me an incredible opportunity. We had rediscovered America's voice in foreign policy. And now it was time for me to leave. In January 2019, I would return to being a private citizen for the first time in fourteen years.

"I want to do something nice for you," he said. "I want to do a press conference or something."

I looked at Jared, hoping he would talk the president out of it. A press conference was unnecessary. The president had already done so much. But Jared agreed with him.

A press conference was not my first concern. It was more important to me that no one know about my resignation until it was officially announced. I didn't want anyone to have the opportunity to pre-spin my departure, I said. There were people in the White House who would take the opportunity to start a rumor that I was leaving because the president and I had had a falling out or some other crazy reason—none of which would be the case. He had been good to me and I knew I had served the country well. I wanted to be able to tell the American people myself why I was resigning.

President Trump said, "Okay. I'll just tell [Chief of Staff John] Kelly." I asked him not to do that. I wanted the news to stay between the three of us in the room. He agreed.

True to his word, the president waited a full week, until the morning of the announcement, to tell the White House staff. I was in Washington, gathering my D.C. staff members to tell them the news. I addressed my staff in New York by videoconference.

My heart hurt telling them about my resignation. Some had sacrificed by moving from South Carolina. Others we were blessed to find when we started our time at the UN. I can't say enough about the people I lovingly refer to as Team Haley. Every day they came to work and literally helped me take on the world. They did it with amazing patriotism, work ethic, and team spirit. They never took their foot off the gas. As I would always say, "We win together, we lose together, and we don't lose." I will forever be grateful for the loyalty of this small but mighty team. They made me better. They had my back. And at the end of the day, each and every one of them is a valued part of our family. I was determined to make sure they each found a new home after the UN. I am proud to say these patriots are still very involved in improving our country, each in his or her own way. Team Haley is spread out now, but they are continuing to make a difference.

By the time I got to the White House for the press conference, the news was everywhere. The announcement caught most people off guard. Calls and texts started coming in from friends and colleagues asking if I was all right. Just as I'd feared, everyone was assuming the worst. I couldn't really blame them. Several members of the administration had exited in less-than-ideal circumstances. It wasn't good for the administration, and it obviously wasn't good for the departing cabinet members. I was thankful to have the opportunity to depart on my own terms.

The president and I were in the Oval Office before the press conference, when he turned to me and asked, "How do you want to do this? Do you want to get a couple podiums?" I replied, "If you're sure you want to do this, I think it should be casual. Just the two of us talking." He agreed. We stayed seated next to each other. We didn't talk beforehand about what we were going to say or how we were going to say it.

President Trump was over-the-top kind in his remarks. He was the man I'd seen many times, the man he too often doesn't let the country see. He praised the progress we'd made in rediscovering America's voice at the UN. He thanked me for our work on North

Korea sanctions. He promised we would stay in touch and graciously said he wanted me to come back into the administration someday.

I thought the president was right. While we were tackling some tough issues around the world, America had a new confidence in the international arena. We were leading again.

"Now the United States is respected," I said. "Countries may not like what we do, but they respect what we do. They know that if we say we're going to do something, we follow it through." I thanked the president and his family for what we accomplished, from cutting $1.3 billion in the UN budget to the South Sudan weapons embargo to moving the U.S. embassy to Jerusalem.

"[T]he U.S. is strong again," I said. "And the U.S. is strong in a way that should make all Americans very proud."

Leaving really wasn't a sudden decision. I knew a few months prior that it would be time to wind down soon. But I kept working at full speed ahead until my last day, so I realized no one would see it coming. Unfortunately, so much of Washington, D.C., is a toxic rumor mill. I knew the key to keeping my integrity and protecting the truth of my good relationship with the president meant controlling the narrative.

"[A] lot of people are going to want to say there's a lot of reasons why I'm leaving. The truth is, I want to make sure this administration, this president, has the strongest person to fight." It had been an intense two years. "I'm a believer in term limits," I said. "I think you have to be selfless enough to know when to step aside and allow somebody else to do that job."

Just before we went to questions from the reporters, I made sure to answer the one question I knew was coming.

"For all of you that are going to ask about 2020: No, I'm not running for 2020," I said. I pointed at President Trump. "I can promise you what I'll be doing is campaigning for this one. So I look forward to supporting the president in the next election."

I SHOULD HAVE KNOWN IT wouldn't be enough.. The next morning, the headline in *The Washington Post* was 'A RISING STAR': HALEY POSES A POTENTIAL THREAT TO TRUMP EVEN IF SHE DOESN'T RUN IN 2020. You can't win with the Washington press corps. The article noted ominously that the "timing of Haley's exit, less than a month before the 2018 midterms, struck many in the president's circle as either savvy or suspect."

Either "savvy or suspect"? Those were my choices? When did we become a country in which the media automatically disregards public officials' explanations for their actions? It reminded me of being called the "A" word—"ambitious." I was being accused of being way more calculating than I am. The truth was, I had been in public service for fourteen years at that point, from the South Carolina legislature to the governorship to the United Nations. I felt it was time for me to take a breath.

What I was thinking about when I announced my intention to resign was neither "savvy" nor "suspect." My only thoughts were about sleeping in, spending more time with my family, finally being able to read books again, and looking forward to Clemson football. I was thinking about not having the stress level I'd endured for over a decade. For the last eight years, seven days a week, twenty-four hours a day, whenever I picked up my phone I had a feeling in the pit of my stomach that bad news was coming. When I resigned, I was looking forward to the day when my phone and I could be friends again.

Some wrote that I was the only departing cabinet member who had left on good terms, with my reputation enhanced by my time in the Trump administration. Usually, when the media wrote those kinds of things, it was more to criticize President Trump than to flatter me. The truth was, if I was leaving the Trump administration in better shape than when I came in, it was because of two things: my good relationship with the president, and my respect for his office.

I think a lot of things accounted for my relationship with the president. But above all, we were able to work together because he trusted me. I understood my job was to carry out his agenda. And he understood that I would always tell him the truth, whether he wanted to hear it or not.

The number-one difference between me and some of those who left the administration on less-than-good terms was that I never thought I was a stand-in for the president. They sometimes did. As a member of the president's cabinet, I conducted myself the same way I wanted my cabinet to treat me when I was governor. I wanted them to be creative. I wanted them to remember that they served the people. And I wanted them to challenge me if they ever thought I was going in a direction they disagreed with. What I did *not* want them to do was to make the mistake of thinking they were the governor, or that they should be. If that's what they sincerely believed, I expected them to resign their positions and take a run at the job themselves.

This was not a question of love of country. Everyone I served with is a patriot. It wasn't even a question of how they felt about the president; some were more on board with his agenda than others. It was a question of following and honoring the Constitution.

At the end of the day, the person who serves as president is the choice of the people. Our job is to serve the people, and that means honoring the office of the presidency. When we think something is wrong, our job is to stand up and make our voices heard. It is not to plot and scheme behind the president's back. We owe our loyalty to the American people and the Constitution.

When my colleagues actively worked to defy the president—and then bragged about it in public, like "Anonymous" did—they broke their trust with the public. They decided *they* were the best judges of who should lead the country, not the people. And they encouraged our adversaries overseas to exploit the instability they created.

There were people in the White House who didn't trust me because I had been critical of the president in the 2016 primary. And there were other people who criticized me for going to work in the Trump administration in the first place. But I wasn't interested in playing political "us versus them" games. I wanted to serve my country with honesty and integrity. In the end, I was blessed to do that.

WHEN I WAS FIRST OFFERED the position of U.S. ambassador to the UN, I half-joked that all I knew about the United Nations was that most Americans didn't like it. I didn't set out as ambassador to change Americans' view of the UN. I set out to show Americans value for their investment in the UN. If I couldn't do that, then I worked to change our investment in the UN.

Some administrations have believed that multilateral institutions like the UN are good in and of themselves, that it is always better for the United States to act together with other nations on the world stage. But the truth is, multilateralism is just a means to an end. It is neither good nor bad—only its *goals and accomplish-ments* are good or bad. Sometimes it is best for the United States to work together with other nations. But sometimes it isn't. When an institution like the UN fails to support our values, we have an obligation to object, and to object loudly.

This is the foundational dilemma of the United Nations. It is set up to treat all countries the same. But all countries are not the same. Some respect freedom and human rights, and some don't. And when you try to pretend there's no difference between these kinds of governments, that's always a win for governments that don't respect human dignity. The Holocaust survivor and Nobel laureate Elie Wiesel put it this way: "Neutrality helps the oppressor, never the victim." He was right.

I watched other administrations refuse to take a stand at the UN and I was determined to do the opposite: I would always be clear about where the United States stood. The United Nations can be a difficult place for moral clarity. So many of the incentives there are for countries to *avoid* taking a stand, to deny that there are universal truths and rights that are the endowment of every human being. Many countries criticize us when we take a stand. But what I learned at the UN is that these countries want the United States to lead. They count on us to lead. Because if we don't stand up for freedom, no one will.

Our values are our most potent foreign-policy tool. They give us leverage at the United Nations and throughout the world. And as long as we are in the UN, we must use them. It's a mistake for the United States to believe we have to go along with the mob in order to be effective. The opposite is true: We have to be the ones to stand up to the mob. When we see rape being used as a weapon of war, dictators getting rich by robbing the people of their resources, or oppressive regimes trying to blame others for the suffering they inflict—when we see these things we have to call them out. When we do, we might not win the vote at the UN, but we can shame these governments. Because when the United States calls out a country or an injustice, the world takes notice.

This goes for our allies, too. Some people wondered why I stood up for Israel so strongly at the UN. The truth is, as much as I admire Israel, I would have stood up for Japan, Australia, Canada, or Great Britain just as much if they needed it. I stood up for Israel because it is a great ally of the United States and because it gets treated so badly at the UN. Being America's friend has to mean something. It has to mean we stand up for our friends; and along with that, we expect our friends to stand up for us.

We have another source of leverage in the international arena, one we should not feel bad about using. We are by far the largest contributor to the United Nations' budget.

Year in and year out, the United States contributes at least 20 percent of the funding for the United Nations system. U.S. taxpayers in places like Oklahoma, Idaho, and Minnesota provide at least 25 percent of the $7 billion budget for UN peacekeeping operations thousands of miles away in Kinshasa, Juba, Pristina, Kosovo, and elsewhere. The American people contribute more than 35 percent of the funding for the world's largest multilateral humanitarian organization, the World Food Program. We contribute 13 percent of the funding that allows UNICEF to help children worldwide. U.S. taxpayers shoulder 42 percent of the burden of paying for the work of the UN Refugee Agency. Don't let anyone tell you America isn't generous in our support of suffering people around the world. It's a false and ungrateful statement. For decades, right up through today, America remains by far the most generous country in the world.

There are times when the American people question our generous support to the United Nations—and for good reason. There are times when we are tempted to believe we could use that money better and more effectively by advancing our principles and interests on our own. Americans have every right to feel this way.

A representative from an African country once lectured me and quoted a biblical passage. He said, "To whom much is given, much is expected." This is certainly true. And the American people have given much. But multilateralism requires that we all contribute, that we all work together for the common good. Everyone has to have skin in the game. Everyone should ultimately benefit. And the goals of multilateralism must be in the American people's interests, and in accord with our values. If they aren't, then we should not participate.

The United States has no expectation of always getting its way in the international arena. But we do have a legitimate expectation to get a return on our investment. Our foreign aid should help the most vulnerable, but it should also serve America's interests. Where we give our money and how much shouldn't be on autopilot. It should go where it can do the most good and where we can expect cooperation and friendship in return.

IN THE PRESS CONFERENCE ANNOUNCING my resignation, I said I would never truly step away from fighting for our country. I meant it. There are issues I have continued to speak out about since I left government. Many of them are issues that involve people and governments overseas, but they also have a strong impact here at home. They are fundamental debates that reflect not just our national interests, but who we are as a country—who we are as a people.

I've been surprised and dismayed at how much time I've spent lately debating a question that I thought was settled decades ago. Young people in the United States are being influenced by liberals on campus, in the media, and in politics to flirt with the idea of socialism. And it's not just on campus. People are being elected to Congress who are doing more than flirting with socialism.

This is an interesting theoretical debate to have, but when you've seen the real world effects of socialism—even initially well-intentioned socialism—the idea that we would adopt this system in the United States is unfathomable.

Socialism in Venezuela began as a popular campaign to put poor people before big corporations. Venezuela had been a democracy, but soon after he was elected, socialist champion Hugo Chávez began to consolidate his power. He packed the courts with his followers. He put his cronies in charge of the critical oil industry. And he justified it all by saying he was delivering socialism to his people. And he got away with it for as long as oil prices were high. But when prices fell, it exposed the damage caused by his economic policies. Basic food items began to disappear from Venezuelan stores.

When Chávez died in 2013 and was succeeded by Nicolás Maduro, the pretense of building a socialist paradise in Venezuela disappeared completely. As the economy continued to crater, Maduro declared capitalists enemies of the state. All the remaining democratic aspects of government were eliminated. Maduro's cronies grew rich through drug trafficking and skimming off food rations for the people.

The result of socialism in Venezuela was that what had once been the wealthiest country in South America became the poorest. In a region where 31 percent of the people are poor, a stunning 90 percent of Venezuelans live below the poverty line. Children are dying of malnutrition. Hospitals are without medicine and supplies. Once eradicated diseases are now reappearing. Venezuelans live in conditions today that they haven't experienced in over one hundred years.

The same story could be told about other countries that have fallen for the cruel hoax presented by socialist politicians. I've seen how socialism destroys freedom, even in those countries that manage to grow their economies off the sweat of their repressed people. And I've seen how it affects these countries' interactions with their neighbors and the world. Take a look at the countries causing the most trouble in the world, and you will see countries that are *not* free. Countries that honor and respect the voices of their people don't threaten peace and security. It's no coincidence that the world has never witnessed a war between two truly free countries.

A good example of the difference between the threat posed by free versus unfree governments is two of the largest- and fastest-growing economies in the world: India and China.

The United States is committed to seeing that Iran never gets a nuclear weapon, because it would be catastrophic for the world. Meanwhile, India is a nuclear power and nobody gives it a second thought. Why? Because India is a democracy and threatens no one.

The United States has a partnership with India that is strong and getting stronger. Our partnership is strategic. Both countries have been the victims of terrorism. We share a commitment to defeating terrorists and the hateful ideology that motivates them. We share a commitment to stopping Afghanistan and Pakistan from giving safe harbor to terrorists, like they did before September 11, 2001.

Most important, our partnership is based on shared principles. Our two countries share a belief in democracy, hard work, family, and achievement. Indian Americans have been very successful in the United States. We are the minority group that is the most educated, has the highest per-capita income, and, most important, is one of the most charitable in America. There are a number of reasons for Indian Americans' success in the United States. But mostly, we're just good at being Americans. And that says as much about America as it does about us.

Contrast our growing partnership with India with the greatest foreign threat the United States faces today: China.

China is working strategically to spread its financial and military presence across the globe—and not in a good way. China steals intellectual property. It helps North Korea cheat on sanctions. The Chinese manipulate their currency in ways that poison our trade relationship. And they are enlarging their military at a rapid pace.

In addition to being a bad economic actor and a strategic threat, the Chinese government is one of the greatest human rights abusers in the world. In their own country it has created "re-education" camps against an ethnic and religious minority, and an Orwellian surveillance state to protect Communist Party control over its people.

It was high time to take a more aggressive approach to U.S. trade with China. I'm not a fan of tariffs. They raise prices for consumers, farmers, and businesses. But I'm grateful that President Trump has taken on China over its trade practices. And I couldn't agree more with his bottom line: We don't want temporary measures from China. We want systematic, verifiable changes in the way it treats American companies and American imports.

Even in China, the limited free-market reforms the government has allowed have had near miraculous results. In 1990, almost 756 million Chinese were living in extreme poverty. By 2015, that number had shrunk to less than 10 million. That is amazing progress, thanks to their embrace of economic freedom. But it is progress that China cannot sustain as long as it continues to micromanage its economy and deny political freedom to its people. The massive protests in Hong Kong in 2019 held an important message for the Chinese regime: Freedom is the yearning of every human heart. Even higher incomes and more consumer goods can't diminish it forever. China is a powerful country, but it is also an unstable one because of the way its government treats its people.

The fact is, the market economy has benefited the entire world, but it has benefited Americans more than most. We all have an obligation to explain to a new generation of Americans how that has happened. We have an obligation to tell them that if you care about global poverty, if you care about childhood disease, literacy, even the environment, you should support capitalism. In the last twenty-five years, over a billion people have raised themselves out of extreme poverty. The World Bank reports that the global poverty rate is at its lowest point in recorded history. That's not the result of socialism. It's because of capitalism.

We all have an obligation to educate young Americans about where socialism leads. Especially those of us who have traveled to countries that claim to be socialist. It leads not just to poverty, but to oppression. It leads to Venezuela. It leads to gulags. America's collective amnesia on this point is becoming a real threat. And it's a threat that comes at us not from abroad, but from within.

ANOTHER ISSUE THAT HAS BOTH foreign and domestic res-onance is immigration. As the daughter of legal immigrants, this issue hits home with me. And whether you're a UN bureaucrat or an American citizen, this debate begins with America's proud immigrant heritage and long-standing moral leadership on this issue. No country has done more than the United States to welcome immigrants and refugees to it shores. And no nation has done more to support migrant and refugee populations across the globe.

In December 2017, I announced that the United States would no longer participate in the drafting of a United Nations document on immigration called the Global Compact for Safe, Orderly and Regular Migration. A lot of commentators immediately concluded that this was yet another anti-immigrant move by the Trump administration. Some reporters even speculated that I had been pressured into ending our participation. It's not true.

The compact grew out of an international statement of principles on migration that had been championed by the Obama administration. The statement was a mess. Like so much of our immigration debate today, it attempted to erase all distinctions between illegal and legal immigration. It also blurred the lines between migrants who choose to leave their countries for economic or family reasons, and refugees whose lives depend on escaping persecution for their race, religion, or other status. But these distinctions are critical. If we no longer acknowledge a difference between legal and illegal immigration—and between people who need international protection and those who just want to escape poverty or crime—we will have a system of completely open immigration. We will have effectively eliminated our borders. We can never do that.

The United States' participation in drafting the compact began under President Obama. When I came into office, we continued to be a part of the debate. Not because we agreed with the principles it was based on, but because we *disagreed* with them. We thought— perhaps naively, in retrospect—that we could improve the compact through our participation. It was a nonbinding, largely symbolic document. We believed that if we could change its language and direction, we could strike a blow for a sane and humane immigration policy. For a time, I wanted to stay in that fight and represent the U.S. viewpoint.

But as the debate went on, it became clear that we couldn't change the outcome. Instead of focusing on the real issues that drive migration—like armed conflict, human rights violations, corruption, and bad economic policy—the document that was emerging focused on issues like climate change. Give me a break. Millions of people didn't flee Syria because of climate change. They fled because chemical bombs were being dropped on their homes by a war-criminal dictator who was clinging to power. Most important, the compact advocated that migration and refugee policy be governed by international law rather than individual countries.

This was a deal breaker. American decisions on immigration policies must always be made by Americans and Americans alone. Only we will decide how best to control our borders and who will be allowed to enter our country. The Global Compact on Migration was headed toward creating an international right to migration, which does not exist in international law and is not compatible with U.S. sovereignty. So we rightly withdrew from the compact. And we were not alone. Australia, Bulgaria, Hungary, Austria, the Czech Republic, Israel, and Poland, among other nations, also either withdrew or abstained from voting.

By the time we withdrew from the agreement, I had met refugees from the war in Syria and from the violence in South Sudan and the Congo. I didn't meet them at a migration conference in New York or Geneva. I met them where they lived, in refugee camps in Turkey, Jordan, and Central Africa. The message of these desperate people was always the same. They wanted to go home. The solution to the global migration crisis was spelled out by President Trump in his 2018 address to the UN General Assembly.

"Ultimately, the only long-term solution to the migration crisis is to help people build more hopeful futures in their home countries," he said. "Make their countries great again."

Here at home, the immigration issue is subject to many of the same distortions. The truth has been horrendously twisted or overlooked entirely. Rights and entitlements for those seeking to come to America are often falsely claimed without any consideration for their impact on the lives of working Americans. Some politicians benefit from the division caused by this debate, so they do what they can to prolong it. Meanwhile, Congress, whose job it is to change the law and fix the situation, does nothing.

I am the proud daughter of Indian immigrants. I don't try to hide that. In fact, I said it just that way in almost every speech I gave as a candidate for governor of South Carolina. I couldn't be prouder of my parents or the journey they made to become Americans. They gave me and my brothers and sister the best possible gift, the gift of living in the greatest country in the world. They reminded us every day how blessed we were to be Americans.

I don't blame people for wanting to come to our country. I welcome it. But we have to be smart about it. We can't let just anyone into our country. We have to vet people for security reasons. We have to prioritize people with skills, not just with family connections. We have to make sure the numbers don't get larger than our ability to absorb. In short, our immigration system is badly broken. Our country will continue to be at odds over this issue until we fix it.

. . .

PRESIDENT TRUMP, IT IS SAID, is the "Disrupter in Chief." We are living through times in which the old Washington, D.C., rule book for politics and government has been thrown out the window. Disruption has benefited our country in many ways. For instance, we now have people in government who understand how business works. They have eliminated miles of red tape that were an obstacle to job creators. And we now have a government that is willing to challenge the foreign-policy establishment. The United States is no longer appeasing the terrorist government in Iran or allowing itself to be taken for granted internationally.

Disrupting the status quo can be valuable. But it also requires a plan for what comes next. The far left has a plan, and it's dangerously wrong. The far left wants to remake America and to undo so much of what has made us great. Its belief is that everything we learned in grade school is wrong. American principles like freedom of speech, religious freedom, and equality before the law don't allow us all to pursue our best lives, it claims. Instead, they protect "privilege."

Support for free speech on college campuses is at dangerous lows. Religious freedom is being trampled in the name of other so-called social-justice goals. And more and more Americans put their fellow Americans into categories based on their race or sexual identity. What so many of us see as rights that benefit everyone, the far left sees as tools that perpetuate inequality. So they must be done away with.

This is deeply misguided. As an Indian American woman, I am keenly aware of the discrimination that has existed and continues to exist in our country. But we mustn't elevate identity politics to the absurd heights that the left takes it. In South Carolina, as in many other parts of America, there are white communities that in many ways are a forgotten part of our country.

Abbeville County, for example, is mostly white, and has a 20 percent poverty rate. It struggles with high rates of drug addiction, domestic violence, and underperforming schools. Few people there fit the stereotypical image of "white privilege." When we have a discussion of race in America, these communities should not be forgotten. We ask them to pay their taxes and fight our wars. We must not also ask them to pay for illegal immigrants' health care and education, or to pay reparations for injustices that their ancestors of eight generations ago might or might not have perpetrated. To truly be one America, we have to include everyone, regardless of race. In some ways we are all victims, but if we dwell on victimhood, we become a nation of grievances, and that undercuts the greatness of America and robs us of a better future.

We don't need to remake America into something different. America isn't perfect, but it is our belief in inalienable rights that has made us the most generous, most prosperous, and most free country in the history of humankind. It is these beliefs that took us from slavery and Jim Crow to electing an African American president. It is the fundamental truth of the Declaration of Independence—that we are all children of God—that allowed my state to go from bitter racial division to coming together to remove a painful symbol of that past. These beliefs have allowed us to achieve a "more perfect Union."

My two years as U.S. ambassador to the United Nations took me to places where these values do not exist, even as an ideal. There is no freedom of speech to appeal to for Venezuelans or Cubans. There was no freedom of religion in Pakistan to protect Asia Bibi when she faced death for the "crime" of being a Christian. There is no equal justice under the law for the Uighurs in China, the Rohingya in Burma, or the Yezidis in Syria.

We don't need a different America. All of us need to show less entitlement and more gratitude for the universal principles that have made our nation great and will make it greater in the future.

CONCLUDING WORDS ARE ALWAYS THE hardest to write. History is easy because facts are real. What comes next is harder. I am an optimist by nature. And I am highly optimistic about America's future. At the same time, I am sobered by the work that remains.

When I came into public office I felt like a rebel. I had defeated the longest-serving member of the South Carolina legislature in a Republican primary. The people of my district took a chance on me. I will forever be grateful to them. But I felt a lot of weight from their choice. South Carolinians had seen how power can make elected officials fearful and complacent. I wanted change. I wanted voices to be heard.

I ran for governor. It didn't make sense for me to run. I had no name recognition and no money. But my team and I had passion, and that means something. I knew if we were given that chance, we could move the ball.

I will leave it to history to judge the difference we made for South Carolina. For my part, I know I left everything on the field. I gave it all I had. I was blessed to serve the state that raised me. If I am remembered for anything, I hope it is that everyone in South Carolina truly understands—whether they agreed with my policies or not—that I did the very best I could to protect them and make their lives better.

Becoming ambassador was a surprise. I certainly didn't expect to be asked, but it was also a defining moment for me. I had so much more I wanted to give. Once again, I was guided by what my parents had always taught us: Whatever you do, be great at it and make sure people remember you for it.

Defending America was in some ways both the hardest and the easiest job I ever had. It was the hardest because every day I felt like I was putting on body armor to go into battle. I knew I would have to fight, I just didn't know which country I would be fighting that day. But in other ways the job was the easiest. America is, hands down, the best country in the world. It was an honor and a privilege to defend her every day.

These days it seems like we're going through growing pains. We judge too quickly. We don't understand our brothers and sisters. Too often we don't even try.

Americans are passionate. We say what we think and we are strong-willed. That will always be one of our strengths. But at some point we need to take a breath. We need to remind each other that we have more in common than we have differences. We need to look at the person who disagrees with us and not see that person as evil but as someone who is a mother, a daughter, a wife, a friend, a professional, and an American.

Wherever I go, I get asked what's next. But I was never the girl who knew exactly who she wanted to be when she grew up. I have always lived for the day. I've always believed that if I made this day a great day, life's doors would open. It has happened so many times in my life. Doors opened, and I found the courage to jump through. And every time I did, I came out stronger on the other side. Everyone needs to remember that when you push through the fear, you change lives. When you pull back, you never know what could have been.

· I truly don't know what's in store for my future. I know that if life stopped for me today, I would feel that I have had a blessed life. The idea that a young Indian girl born of immigrants in a small rural town would grow up to be governor of her state and U.S. ambassador to the United Nations is blessing enough. I will never want more, because I have lived a life that's unimaginable. I thank God every night for the many blessings in my life. And for me, that's enough. If God has another door for me, He will show it.

I realize there are many who will think this book is motivation for something in the future. I can't help that. I can only say that facts are remembered and emotions fade, but it is the emotions that dictate the lessons we learn. I wanted all of you to know what I felt as I went through these times in my life.

I don't know what's next, but I've learned some things along the way that will help me find it:

First, I know I carry a burden of gratitude. My parents sacrificed so much for their children. I have met people all over the world who sacrifice as well. I know the blessings I have been given. I will always continue to give back in some way.

Second, it's the simple things that make life worth living. So be kind. Don't judge. Push through the fear. And laugh every chance you get, because you will be challenged.

And should life get dicey, I have a couple surefire strategies for coping. You can say almost anything with both strength and dignity if you start with, "With all due respect." And a well-timed "Bless your heart" will keep your enemies guessing.

So live your life with grit and grace. Count your blessings. Love your family. And remember: Even on our worst days, we are blessed to live in America.

Acknowledgments

There is something about writing a book. It is very therapeutic in that it combines facts with emotions and allows you to reconcile the two. I feel a great deal of gratitude to those who have helped me, both with this process and in my journey so far.

I have been blessed beyond measure to be able to serve the state that raised me and to represent the country I love so much. None of this would be possible without the strong love and support of my family.

Michael, as you know, I am never at a loss for words, but I am when it comes to thanking you. We have literally grown up together. Through it all you have loved me, had my back, and held my hand when it felt like no one else would. Marrying you will continue to be the best decision I have ever made. Thank you for being my best friend and making life fun. I love you.

Rena and Nalin, I'm so proud to be your mom. My heart is full just thinking of you. I know public life hasn't been easy, but you have never complained. You have understood we are a family of service. You have both grown to be amazing people and made us so proud. I love you, too.

Thank you to my amazing parents, Ajit and Raj Randhawa. Everything I am is because of how you both raised me. Mom, I learned my strength and courage from you. Dad you taught me the importance of kindness and grace. I will always be proud to be your daughter.

The only thing better than one set of amazing parents is two! To my second set, Bill and Carole Haley, thank you for your constant love and support. But more important, thank you for giving me Michael. I am thankful every day for both of you and the genuine love you have always shown me.

I loved being one of four kids. It always felt like a party. Thank you to my brothers and my sister for putting up with having to answer for me. A special thanks goes to my brother Mitti for being the best older brother a girl could ever have. I could make the most embarrassing mistake, and you would find a way to make me feel like I was great. I will always think you hang the moon.

To my dear friend Jon Lerner. It's hard to describe the appreciation I have for you. From taking a chance on me in my run for governor, to working with me at the United Nations, to helping me with this book, I am beyond grateful to you. Your advice and counsel have always been spot on. More than that, your friendship is one I will always value. Thank you for the trust, loyalty, laughs, and the reminder that there are good people in politics.

To my sweet friends on "Team Haley": From South Carolina to the United Nations to Stand for America, you have always been the reason for my success. Each and every one of you has a special place in my heart. To my security-detail family, thank you for taking care of our family. We will always consider you as part of ours. You made stressful times fun and you never let your guard down. I always knew "you had me," and for that I will always be grateful. Signing off from G1 and Pathfinder with great love for you all.

To my team, thank you. Thank you for the friendship, the loyalty, and making this crazy life fun. Each of you has contributed so much to your state and country. I hope you will forever be proud of your mark on improving the lives of people, because I will always be proud of you. Once a member of Team Haley, always a member of Team Haley.

To Jessica Gavora: The United Nations and now two books together warrants you a special badge. Your ability to capture my words and emotions is exceptional. From my crazy emails in the middle of the night to my changing until the last second, you are a true professional. I am blessed that I found you. Thank you for your friendship.

To my sweet friend, Bob Barnett, I still want to be you when I grow up! Thank you for not letting me fall. Your experience and counsel is the best. And, yes, you were right.

To George Witte and our friends at St. Martin's Press, thank you for making writing this book a fun experience. You have been fantastic partners in helping me tell my story.

To the people of my home state, it will always be a great day in South Carolina. I am so very proud to be a daughter of our state. Thank you for taking a chance on me and allowing me to serve you.

Finally, to all of my brothers and sisters in our great country: Thank you for the privilege and honor to serve the best country in the world. You made this small-town girl dream of something bigger than herself.

Index